Sebastian Masuda

FASHION AUTEURS

Series Editors
Adam Geczy and Vicki Karaminas

Fashion Auteurs is a groundbreaking book series devoted to designers who have left an indelible mark on fashion history. Critical, clear and concise, each title, comprising around 30K words, is written by authorities in the field, situating each designer within their time and against their peers, with a focus on the contributions that have made them memorable. Using the term 'auteur' to designate film directors with a distinctive and influential style, this is the first series to treat fashion designers and related fashion creators (e.g. photographers) as on par with artists who have decisively shaped imagery, taste, and what is seen to be current and desirable. These books will be of interest not only to fashionistas and ardent devotees of fashion magazines but also to students and teachers of art and design, artists and designers themselves, not to mention anyone seeking a deeper acquaintance with fashion and design culture.

Forthcoming Titles in the Series
Judith Beyer, *Alessandro Michele*
Benjamin Wild, *Thom Browne*

Sebastian Masuda

Yuniya Kawamura

ANTHEM PRESS

Anthem Press
An imprint of Wimbledon Publishing Company
www.anthempress.com

This edition first published in UK and USA 2026
by ANTHEM PRESS
75–76 Blackfriars Road, London SE1 8HA, UK
or PO Box 9779, London SW19 7ZG, UK
and
244 Madison Ave #116, New York, NY 10016, USA

© 2026 Yuniya Kawamura

The author asserts the moral right to be identified as the author of this work.

All rights reserved. Without limiting the rights under copyright reserved above,
no part of this publication may be reproduced, stored or introduced into
a retrieval system, or transmitted, in any form or by any means
(electronic, mechanical, photocopying, recording or otherwise),
without the prior written permission of both the copyright
owner and the above publisher of this book.

British Library Cataloguing-in-Publication Data
A catalogue record for this book is available from the British Library.

Library of Congress Cataloging-in-Publication Data: 2025938415
A catalog record for this book has been requested.

ISBN-13: 978-1-83999-537-8 (Hbk) / 978-1-83999-538-5 (Pbk)
ISBN-10: 1-83999-537-8 (Hbk) / 1-83999-538-6 (Pbk)

This title is also available as an eBook.

In Memory of Yoya Kawamura

CONTENTS

List of Figures and Table — xi

Preface — xv

Introduction: Sebastian Masuda: the Godfather of the Japanese Kawaii Culture — xix

1. The Childhood and Adolescent Years: Questioning What "Normal" Means — 1
2. The Start of 6%DOKIDOKI in Harajuku — 27
3. Exporting the Kawaii Aesthetic from Harajuku to the World — 59
4. A New Chapter in New York and Beyond — 91

Conclusion: Painting and Energizing the Kawaii World with Colors — 105

Appendix A — 109

Appendix B — 123

References — 125

Index — 131

LIST OF FIGURES AND TABLE

1.1.	Masuda at the age of four with his grandmother (1974); Photo courtesy of Sebastian Masuda	3
1.2.	Masuda at the age of three with his mother (1973); Photo courtesy of Sebastian Masuda	4
2.1.	Masuda at the age of twenty-seven inside 6%DOKIDOKI shop (1997); Photo by Shoichi Aoki, *FRUiTS* Magazine	32
2.2.	Shopgirls as models in 6%DOKIDOKI apparel brand (2024); Photo by Alvaro Nates, AXEL ESCALANTE	45
2.3.	"A Mountain of Memories" at the FOREVER COLORS Exhibition (2019) at A/D Gallery in Roppongi; Photo courtesy of Sebastian Masuda Studio	47
2.4.	"Unforgettable Tower" at the 60th Anniversary SANRIO Exhibition: The Beginning of KAWAII (2021); Photo courtesy of Sebastian Masuda Studio	48
2.5.	"Polychromatic Skin -Gender Tower-" (2022) at the Roppongi Art Night; Photo Courtesy of Sebastian Masuda Studio	49
2.6.	Kyary Pamyu Pamyu's "PONPONPON" music video (2011); Photo courtesy of Sebastian Masuda Studio	51

2.7.	The Melty Room at KAWAII MONSTER CAFE in Harajuku (2015); Photo courtesy of Sebastian Masuda Studio	53
3.1.	"Melty-Go-Round-Harajuku Girl-", a permanent installation, at the Japan Pavillion, Epcot Center, Disney World in Florida (since 2015); ©Disney, All Rights Reserved	67
3.2.	6%DOKIDOKI Fashion Show in Toronto, Canada (2019); Photo courtesy of 6%DOKIDOKI	69
3.3.	"Colorful Rebellion -Seventh Nightmare-" Exhibition (2014) in New York; Photo by GION	70
3.4.	A giant Hello Kitty statue for "Time After Time Capsule" (2015) in New York; Photo by Yusuke Sakamoto	75
3.5.	"Yes, Kawaii Is Art-EXPRESS YOURSELF-" (2024) at Japan House Los Angeles; Photo by Kaori Suzuki	77
3.6.	Masuda at SUSHIDELIC in NY (2023); Photo by Naoyasu Mera	79
3.7.	Shopgirls in 6%DOKIDOKI brand (2024); Photo courtesy of 6%DOKIDOKI	87
4.1.	Masuda Strolling in Lower East Side, NY (2023); Photo courtesy of Sebastian Masuda Studio	95
4.2.	Masuda preparing for the COLORS FOR PEACE Exhibition in NY (2023); Photo courtesy of Sebastian Masuda Studio	98

4.3. Masuda with his followers in Decora fashion at the COLORS FOR PEACE Exhibition reception in NY (2023); Photo by GION   99

Table

3.1. Locations and Dates of the Time After Time Capsule Installations   74

PREFACE

This book commemorates the thirtieth anniversary of Sebastian Masuda's iconic shop and apparel brand, 6%DOKIDOKI, which were launched in Harajuku in 1995 when he was twenty-five years old. It was a pure coincidence that I found Masuda's interview video online a couple of years ago. I knew he was an influential member of the Harajuku's kawaii community and fashion characterized by kaleidoscopic colors, but I had never had a chance to meet him in person or interview him during my fieldwork research on Japanese youth subcultures in Tokyo more than a decade ago. I found out in the video clip that he has relocated from Tokyo and is now a resident of New York as I am. I decided to invite him to my class at Fashion Institute of Technology (FIT), where I teach, as a guest speaker during the spring 2024 semester and asked him to introduce Harajuku and give a lecture on his design philosophy and artwork to my students. He generously offered his time. That was our first encounter and the start of our communication and dialogue. I have always been fascinated with Japanese youth subcultures with distinct aesthetic expressions found on the streets of

Harajuku, which is now a globally famous neighborhood that produces unique styles. Masuda is one of the important and major creators and producers of the kawaii culture that is spreading throughout the world.

When Anthem Press asked me to write a biographical account of a Japanese designer of my choice, Masuda's name immediately came to my mind. Fashion scholars tend to focus more on the Japanese designers who became successful in Paris in the 1970s and 1980s and pay less attention to the ones who have made a significant impact on subcultural youth fashion; they are often left aside or untouched because their styles are far from luxury high fashion shown on the catwalks of Paris or New York Fashion Week. However, the more I talked to Masuda in person, researched about him and his work, and reviewed a long list of his exceptional and remarkable accomplishments in the past decade both domestically and internationally, the more I felt he deserved recognition from the global fashion research community. He was chosen by Newsweek Japan in 2019 as one of the hundred most respected Japanese in the world; he was appointed as a cultural envoy by the Japanese Agency of Cultural Affairs in 2017 and a visiting professor at New York University between 2017 and 2018. He has been making a major contribution not only to the fashion and art industry but also to Japan's cultural diplomacy through his activities using vibrant colors as his creative foundation.

Masuda is a globe trotter and receives invitations to events and conferences around the world so I had to find time to squeeze in my one-on-one interviews with him in-between his packed schedule. There are many essays, stories and anecdotes written about him in English, Japanese, and many other languages, but this book is the first full biographical account of Masuda distributed throughout the world as a print and electronic publication in English. I feel very privileged and honored to write a book about him and his life journey.

My gratitude goes to Adam Geczy at the University of Sydney in Australia and Vicki Karaminas at the Massey University in New Zealand, the two editors of the *Fashion Auteurs* series, who invited me and gave me the opportunity to participate in their project, and my thanks also go to the editorial, marketing, and production teams at Anthem Press who made the publishing process as efficient as possible. I am also thankful to Mika Kitamura, Masuda's manager and right arm, who has been extremely cooperative and generously provided me with the photos used in this book. Lastly, I owe a special debt of gratitude to Sebastian Masuda who offered his time to meet with me in New York and Tokyo amid his incredibly busy schedule so that I could complete this book. Without his cooperation, this book would not have been possible.

I am sure the readers will understand the concept and depth of kawaii through his activities and accomplishments both in Japan and around the world, which is often misunderstood as something that is simply childish and infantile. Kawaii, which is translated as cute in English, is not merely an adjective but is an ideology, philosophy, and lifestyle with multiple layers of deep and intricate meanings. The colors have the power to change not only one's personality but also attitudes toward life; they can also save a person. Some of his dedicated followers may relate to his difficult and complex childhood and adolescent years which he rarely talks about in public. Those who are not familiar with his work will be inspired by the way he paints and energizes the world with psychedelic, neon colors which are now his artistic weapon.

Yuniya Kawamura
New York and Tokyo
March 2025

Introduction

SEBASTIAN MASUDA: THE GODFATHER OF THE JAPANESE KAWAII CULTURE

This book is a biographical account of Sebastian Masuda's life and work. It examines how he rose from a child born with a hearing impairment to a respected and celebrated designer and creator. He is known as the Godfather of the Japanese kawaii[1] (cute) culture originated in Harajuku, one of Japan's most famous fashionable districts, in addition to Shibuya, Shinjuku, and Ginza. Harajuku is home to many youth subcultures, such as Lolita, Decora, and streetwear, and it is a mecca for subcultural followers and enthusiasts. Masuda attributes his artistic skills, creativity, and the use of unique color combinations to his hearing difficulty earlier in his life, which was suddenly cured by the time when he was six years old. Because he could not hear for the first several years of his life, his visions were more sensitive and acute than those who could hear, and his visual stimulations were much stronger than others. He strongly believes that what he is today is because of everything he had gone through as a child, as well as his unconventional upbringing and family background. As long as he could remember, he did not want to have a child of his own so that he could cut off the biological family lineage and would not reproduce the same kind of emotional instability, insecurity, and distress that he and his siblings[2] had experienced while growing up. A safety net for psychological and economic protection that a family normally provided to their children was gradually lost in his family.

Immersing himself in the art and theater world as an adolescent before Masuda opened his shop, 6%DOKIDOKI, was an escape from his depressing reality, and making artwork was a cathartic and therapeutic experience because he could eliminate all the distractions from his head and give his full attention to what he was doing. He explained his creative process to me[3]:

> I like to make things. I am not the type who just throws out an abstract concept and have other people do it for me. I do it myself, or even if I ask others to create some parts of the project, I want to be able to give specific and detailed instructions. I am involved in all of the projects. I am the one who provides a design foundation, and I rely on my staff to do the rest. And that sometimes leads to a very creative object that I never thought of making so their creativity is also added on to my creative ideas. People

often think that I first draw a rough sketch, but my method is different. I begin my designing process with words or sentences. Written words are visual images to me. I build my visual designs based on these written words.

He writes down words and sentences and executes them into visual designs. Thoughts and emotions are sometimes difficult to verbalize for the youths, so he feels that it is his job and responsibility to make their voices that are hidden and covered heard. Since visual designs function as a nonverbal mode of communication, he represents the words of the youths who have the urge to say something and are eager to let out their anxiety, insecurity, anger, and fear. Among the multiple titles that Masuda carries is "a magician of colors." His preference for bright colors is traced back to his childhood years. The vibrant colors used in his works are mainly derived from the shopping arcade in his hometown, Matsudo. As a child, he walked around the arcade after school with the allowance that his parents gave him to buy snacks and toys in bright, colorful packages, and they were engrained in his memory.[4]

I trace Masuda's life chronologically so that readers will understand where he started from, how he was raised, what his upbringing was like, why he got obsessively involved in the underground art and theater world, when he launched his shop, how he had achieved his international success and fame, and why he decided to relocate to New York in 2022 and added his creative base there.

Chapter 1 begins with his early childhood years with hearing difficulty and examines his family that ran a kimono shop during Japan's most prosperous years in the 1980s. It also traces Masuda's maternal family background that he believes might have affected the family that the mother had procreated. It also addresses his adolescent years when he began spending more and more time with his friends in Harajuku on weekends and stayed away from home. After graduating from high school, moving to Osaka and returning to his hometown, he was deeply involved in the Japanese avant-garde, underground art and theater community that was extremely popular at the time among the youths who were feeling lost, and his participation in the community later influenced his creative endeavors. Not being accepted by and having no attachment to his family, school, and mainstream society has shaped his views on life because he was able to subconsciously provide a space literally and metaphorically to those who were similar to him and had no sense of belonging in and little attachment to their surroundings. He created an environment that was warm, accepting, and nonjudgmental, and welcomed anyone on the social periphery without any prejudice or preconceived biases.

Chapter 2 focuses on his shop, 6%DOKIDOKI, which became a hangout for many youths, and its reputation spread so widely that celebrities from overseas, such as Sofia Coppola and Niki Minaj, visited it. Out of all other fashion districts in Tokyo, such as Shibuya and Shinjuku, he chose Harajuku for his first shop.[5] DOKIDOKI, an onomatopoeia in Japanese that mimics the noise, is a term for the heartbeat that expresses one's excitement and nervousness at the same time.[6] Some of the girls who used to hang out and worked in his shop are now globally known entertainers, such as Kyary Pamyu Pamyu and Mizyu, a member of Atarashii Gakko.[7] He initially planned to sell secondhand clothes imported from the US, but his trip to the US accidentally took a different turn. Having his own shop as a base, Masuda was creating a new subculture called Decora, which was never his intention or goal; it emerged organically. A subculture provides a physical and psychological space to those who do not have a place that they feel comfortable or safe in.

Chapter 3 addresses his creative ideas that are rooted in traditional Japanese philosophy and explores his global popularity as a designer and creator, which started with the World Tour in 2009 when he was invited to visit Paris. Since then, he never lets any chances slip away even if he was not ready to take on some new projects. He and his team continue to organize fashion shows, give lectures, and set up pop-up stores at different conventions. He also attends overseas conferences and organizes installations and exhibitions in New York, Los Angeles, Amsterdam, and London, among many other cities. He has earned recognition not only from the fashion community but also from the Japanese government and the academic community. He was appointed as a cultural envoy and a visiting professor. He has made a contribution to the dissemination of Japan's soft power that is used as part of

Japan's cultural diplomacy. He is also active in charity projects and takes fundraising and donations very seriously.

Chapter 4 discusses how his life has come full circle. Moving to New York was his long-term goal since he wanted to establish another creative base overseas in addition to Harajuku. It was delayed for a few years because of the COVID-19 pandemic, but he had finally arrived in New York in February 2022. He humbly accepts that he is a newcomer to the city and solves problems and challenges as they come along. He has turned a new page in his life in his 50's, while other Japanese men in his generation are already planning retirement.

Much has been written about Masuda in print and online, but no scholar has ever traced his life story or written about him in depth from his childhood until the present. This book is based on both primary and secondary information about Masuda. I have interviewed him in person on a number of occasions; he has come to my class at FIT as a guest speaker, and I have also confirmed some of the stories and anecdotes that he had included in his autobiography published in Japanese in 2011 and 2018[8]; I have reviewed countless interview articles in both online and print magazines and watched YouTube videos. I had the opportunity to visit his exhibition in Los Angeles in the fall of 2024 and attended a live conversation he had with Professor James Meraz of ArtCenter College of Design in Pasadena, CA. He invited me to visit his shop and meet his staff members in Tokyo during the summer of 2024. I am using the term "kawaii" with a lowercase "k" as an English adjective and noun throughout the book unless it is used as a proper noun in the project or exhibition titles.

This book will surely be picked up by Masuda's devoted fans and loyal followers who adore, worship, and respect his artwork and him as a designer and creator who represents their voices and feelings they have toward the world. It will also attract those who are interested in joining any subcultural or countercultural group. It is not just a life story of Masuda, but it is also a textbook for those who find it difficult to fit into this complex society where people appear to be deeply connected in the virtual space but at the same time are also disconnected in their personal and non-virtual life. The digital communication provides an illusion that they are psychologically very close, but in fact, they are not. Having a sense of belonging defines one's identity, but it was something that Masuda struggled to find in his younger days. His experience is surely relatable to many around the world, and they can identify themselves with him. He is a spokesperson and representative for today's youths who will realize through this book that they are not alone. They live in a society full of dilemmas, contradictions, and hypocrisies. Many readers will be inspired by Masuda's philosophy and ideology and have much to learn from his work. This book will also be of interest to scholars who are interested in designers and creators as the authors of their own life.

Masuda believes that it is necessary to trace his family roots to better understand where an individual's problems come from and why some are hopelessly incurable. He knows it firsthand.

Although it may be incredibly difficult to investigate the cause, it is important to dig deep into it in order to better investigate the origin of the problem. The stories he shared and provided for this book are candid, honest, truthful, moving, and at times, painful, and heartbreaking. Masuda is a man of integrity, determination, and perseverance.

Notes

1. See "Kawaii as the Aesthetic Movement in Harajuku" in Chapter 2.
2. Masuda is the oldest of the three, with a younger sister and brother.
3. Interview with the author in New York on April 8, 2024.
4. Nanae Mizushima, "No. 97 Interview: Sebastian Masuda-Kawaii Is a Concept, and Not About Things," *Roppongi Mirai Kaigi*, September 26, 2018. https://6mirai.tokyo-midtown.com/en/interview/97/.
5. He used to have several shops throughout Japan, but he decided to concentrate on the one in Harajuku and closed all others because he felt his main theme was being lost.
6. See Chapter 2. Masuda explains how he came up with the name 6%DOKIDOKI.
7. Kyary Pamyu Pamyu is a Japanese model and singer who made a debut in 2011; see Chapter 2. Atarashii Gakko is a Japanese vocal and dance performance girls group known in Japan as "Atarashii Gakko No Leaders." Both have reached the international audience and are globally popular.
8. Sebastian Masuda, *Kakeizu Katta* (*The Family Tree Cutter*) (Kadokawa Publishing, 2011); Sebastian Masuda, *Sekai ni Hitotsudake no Kawaii no Mitsuke Kata* (*How to Find Only One "Kawaii" in the World*) (Sunmark Publishing, 2018).

Chapter 1

THE CHILDHOOD AND ADOLESCENT YEARS: QUESTIONING WHAT "NORMAL" MEANS

If the definition of a normal and traditional family in Japanese mainstream society is a two-parent household with a father who is a breadwinner and protects his wife and children by taking full responsibility for financial matters in the household, and a mother who cooks every day and makes bento boxes for her children[1] and handles all the domestic chores while making sure that her children are well taken care of and they safely come home every night, Masuda's family and upbringing were far from normal, to say the least. In order to escape from his family, he began to spend time in Harajuku as a teenager and immersed himself in the underground art and theater community. His artistic endeavors never received favorable reviews, but he was able to turn a negative into a positive in his later years. In order to understand how he got to where he is today as an internationally acclaimed designer and artist who travels the world, this chapter traces his childhood and adolescent years prior to the launch of his shop, 6%DOKIDOKI in Harajuku, when he spent his days questioning what a normal family entails or means.

The Childhood Years with a Hearing Impairment

Masuda was the first grandchild in the family and was a spoiled child, especially by his grandmother, who was living with him and his parents (Figures 1.1 and 1.2). He was born in Matsudo,[2] Chiba, in 1970; he spent his childhood and teenage years during Japan's unprecedented economic prosperity in the early- to mid-1980s.[3] His parents owned a kimono shop that his grandmother started. This was when Japanese consumers had a lot of disposable income and were spending money on luxury items, such as expensive kimono, jewelry, imported cars, and real estate. His parents' shop sold high-quality kimonos like hot pancakes, and they were incredibly busy running the shop; the mother was attending to the customers while the father was delivering kimonos to their affluent customers. In the meantime, Masuda and his siblings were left on their own. The uphill economy seemed like a never-ending euphoria that Japanese people were experiencing at the time. But it did not last forever, and neither did their kimono shop. As their business began to crumble, so did their family.

THE CHILDHOOD AND ADOLESCENT YEARS

Figure 1.1. Masuda at the age of four with his grandmother (1974); Photo courtesy of Sebastian Masuda.

Figure 1.2. Masuda at the age of three with his mother (1973); Photo courtesy of Sebastian Masuda.

In his painfully candid autobiography which he published in Japanese, he explains the need to trace his family lineage so that he can understand how and where all the family problems started from.[4] He makes a very powerful statement at the very beginning of the book: "Ever since I was in my teens, I swore to myself that I will never have a child of my own."[5] The reason is to sever the biological family lineage and to make sure all the misfortunes that had happened in his family would never be reproduced or replicated. As a child, he always questioned whether the problems his family were facing were curable or not which he later came to a conclusion although it took a while for him to find the conclusion.

The family

While Masuda's parents were running and managing a lucrative kimono shop that catered to wealthy clients, it was his grandmother and housekeepers who mostly took care of him and his siblings. He remembered doing things that he should not have done, but he was much aware as a child that his parents would not dare scold him or say anything to him because of the sense of guilt they had for not being able to spend quality time with their children and provide them with a normal family life, such as having a dinner together or going out together on weekends. As a young boy, Masuda knew that being a child was an advantage and an asset he could use and exploit. His parents made a bank account in his name and saved money for his future. When he was in the second grade in elementary school, he stole the bank card from the drawer, went to the bank and withdrew money, lots of money, from the account. The bankers thought he was there on behalf of his parents. In fact, he was simply stealing the money. He repeated this over and over again and used up all the money that his parents had saved for his college education, but no one in the family ever expressed any concerns.

The kimono shop was financially supported by the grandmother's wealthy patron. She was his mistress, and Masuda's mother was born out of wedlock. The two women, the grandmother and mother, were extremely well taken care of by the patron who provided them with a comfortable living so initially, they never had to face any financial difficulties. Masuda's mother was told that her father died a long time ago when she was little, which she never doubted. But accidentally, she found out that her mother was a mistress to a man who used to visit the shop frequently. It shattered Masuda's mother psychologically into pieces, and from that day onward, she became emotionally unstable and verbally and physically abusive. In a society where the rate of single-parent households headed by mothers is extremely low compared to two-parent households, not having a father is an unspeakable and outrageous social stigma, especially in the 1950s and 1960s, so it continued to haunt her until her adult years. The grandmother who did not know how to handle his daughter's misery, began to rely on faith in God looking for solace and comfort.

Later in life, Masuda's mother met a man who was from a well-to-do family, and they fell in love, but when it was time for him to discuss marriage, the man's family found out that she was born out of wedlock so they were forced to break up. This was another mental blow to her, and it again broke her emotionally. She then met another man who later became her husband, that is, Masuda's father, and he agreed to carry the wife's last name and promised to run the kimono business with her and her mother.[6] She was married at the age of twenty-one and was eager to create a happy and warm family with two parents and children in the household that she had never had while growing up. Masuda was born as the oldest of three children, and the birth of her first child was supposed to be the start of a normal family and become a good, nurturing mother. However, she probably did not know the meaning and definition of a good mother; she never did any domestic chores for her family that were supposed to be done by a normal mother. All the domestic tasks, such as cleaning, washing dishes, laundry, cooking, and changing the baby's diapers were done by the housekeepers that they had hired since she was too busy running the kimono shop. She never cooked. Unlike ordinary young Japanese women who learn to cook, she never learnt how to cook even after she was married. When she made an attempt to cook, she was a hopeless cook. Masuda's bento box was edible but simple, to put it mildly: rice with French fries, rice with sliced apples, or rice with a frozen hamburger patty. His classmates' bento boxes were more elaborate and different. It was clearly apparent that their mothers had spent time to prepare their lunch. People realize what is normal or not normal when they have something to compare it with, and they acquire a sense of inferiority or superiority by finding out where exactly they stand in a normal society that has social differences, and that is how they gauge whether they are better or worse than their peers. In Masuda's case, the bento box and the dishes on the dinner table at his friend's house were shockingly different from what he had in his household, and that sent him a powerful message. He gradually came to see and realize what was not normal about his family.

Hearing impairment

In the midst of his family's extremely hectic life, it took the family a while to find out that their first-born child had no hearing.[7] Masuda as a young boy went through multiple medical tests, and it turned out that his ear canals were very narrow which prevented him from having a normal audible ability. And the doctor suggested that it would be difficult for him to be in the same school with ordinary kids since he could not hear so the parents should consider sending him to a special education school. They decided to perform a surgery on his ears so that his hearing could improve, and the date for the ear operation was set. Masuda's mother prayed and prayed for the success of the surgery, and then on that same night, all of a sudden, Masuda could hear the sound of the wind blowing and shouted out loud, "It's too noisy!" His hearing had miraculously recovered to the point that the surgery was no longer necessary. The mother was stunned and amazed at the power of her prayers and how the prayers could answer her wishes and solve problems. This was how, like his grandmother, she began to rely on a spiritual faith. She believed strongly that prayers have the power to heal and cure which is something that Masuda himself completely dismisses. Her life began to revolve around the faith throughout Masuda's adolescent and adult years.[8]

The trauma reenactment in the Masuda family

Masuda, who is a well-read and observant individual, carefully and objectively analyzed his family's ordeal. He questioned many times why his parents were never able to create a normal, happy family and self-analyzed and wrote in his autobiography that he came to the conclusion that this seemed to stem from what is called "trauma reenactment" in psychology.[9] This is why he had decided a long time ago that he would never have children of his own.

Although the grandmother was financially well taken care of, it was not exactly a conventional structure of a family without a male figure in the family since a normal Japanese family is always patriarchal with a male head. Having a mother who was never married and having been born out of wedlock, are nothing to be proud of in Japanese society, especially in those days, and that was why the mother was never told that her mother was unmarried and Masuda's mother was born out of wedlock. The family would have kept it a secret as long as possible or forever if it were never uncovered. The father used to frequently visit the shop, played with her and take good care of her, but she did not know that this man was in fact her biological father.

According to Sigmund Freud (1886–1939), an Austrian German psychoanalyst, human beings have the innate drive to recreate an event repeatedly, and these events often come from the most painful situations from their childhood and end up performing a new version of an old familiar event that they had gone through.[10] The psychoanalytical theory explains that when early attachment trauma is reenacted, it is often based on intergenerational transmission of abuse, neglect, abandonment, or betrayal, and similarly, people are drawn toward something that is familiar and therefore, comfortable, even if it gives a negative impact on their emotional health. Since there is a compulsion to repeat,[11] if Masuda were to have a family and children of his own, there is a strong possibility that the same tragic events are reenacted, according to the theory of trauma reenactment. People learn the methodologies to create or not create a happy family while growing up. If one came from a warm family, one would know how to reproduce it since the process has been learnt. The reverse could also be true. If people have experienced and witnessed traumatic events in the family, they unfortunately know the process of producing and reproducing it. Masuda, as a perceptive and insightful individual, did not wish to take that risk because what he knew and was familiar with was the latter.

The Adolescent Years: A Deep Sense of Failure

By the time Masuda was a teenager, Japan's economy was starting to decline and was entering into recession. For the first time in Japanese history, the lifetime employment system was starting to crumble. Companies could no longer keep incompetent employees simply out of generosity and sympathy. Middle-aged men who had vowed to dedicate their lives to one company were getting fired. This was when the suicide rates among middle-aged men soared, the divorce rates increased, mothers who used to be homemakers now had to find employment to supplement household income, and students started to drop out of schools not being able to pay tuition.[12] The idea of conformity as Japanese society's central value was thrown out of the window, and people were losing a sense of attachment and belonging. Masuda was no exception. He was a lost teenager who did not know what he wanted to do in life, wandering from place to place, and friends to friends, which many youths can relate to today. The youths who acted out their rage, anger, and hatred, subconsciously knew what they were doing or saying had no meaning, substance, significance, or weight in society, and wondered how their future life was going to turn out. They needed something exciting and entertaining to fill a void in their heart.

Highschool days in Harajuku

Since his high school days, Masuda started going to Harajuku to get away from his dysfunctional family and parents who were always fighting. He was sick of everything and everyone around him. Every Saturday night, he took the last train bound for Tokyo from his hometown in Chiba. His family never asked where he was going or what time he would be home. They were rather indifferent to what he was doing. He was free, but freedom also coincided with loneliness. The train carts were totally empty. It took about an hour to get to Omotesando which is a walking distance to Harajuku, and then he walked to Shibuya which was and is a very exciting and attractive neighborhood for those who want to act cool and grow up quickly so that they are old enough to get away from their families, and Masuda was one of them. There was a spot, in front of a store, where they all met before they ventured out to the streets. Like Masuda's childhood days when he was secretively withdrawing and stealing money from the bank account, he and his friends stole bottles from a box of liquor bottles placed in front of a pub or a restaurant, and this was when Masuda learnt how to steal, drink, and smoke. He knew that these guys he was hanging out with were good for nothing, but it was far better and more comfortable than staying at home with his family. He hated staying at home and being in school. He had a strong resentment towards adults because they were all liars. But at the same time, he wondered how long he would last being with those losers that he was hanging out with. He was looking at his own self with a logical mind, and he intuitively knew he would eventually get out of the group to make something out of his life. This was a fake and superficial camaraderie and friendship that were created through delinquent and illegal activities. There was nothing positive and constructive about what he was doing, and he was very much aware of the fact that it was criminal.

Moving to Osaka and back to Chiba

After graduating from high school, the friends whom he used to hang out with in Harajuku and Shibuya were getting involved in shady and illegal business which Masuda did not want any part of. He was constantly questioning himself, "what am I doing here?" and "what am I achieving with those guys?" He needed to get out. And the easiest and most plausible explanations to leave the community without creating any commotion was to say that he was leaving Tokyo to study in Osaka. That was the reason why he went to Osaka to enroll himself into an art and design school. His parents agreed to pay for his tuition and living. But despite their expectations, it did not work out. There were some discrepancies in his admission application, and it was returned to him. He never corrected it and resubmitted it.

Masuda was stuck in a new city where he did not know anyone and did not have any connections. He tried a number of part-time jobs here and there, but that also did not work out. He was always making mistakes and being yelled at. Not being able to speak the Osaka dialect, which is quite different from the Tokyo dialect considered standard Japanese, they could easily tell that Masuda was an outsider and not a local. The culture of Osaka is very different from that of Tokyo. He simply did not fit in and was not able to assimilate into their culture; there was a deep sense of being excluded, unneeded and unwanted. He more or less became a *hikikomori*, a social recluse who does not work or go to school and stays in their room all day; it is a form of severe social withdrawal, which is a major social problem and phenomenon in Japan.[13]

Not having much to do, he began going to a local library in Osaka every day, just randomly picking out books to read. He read and read every day from morning to night. Then someone in the library noticed that he was always there reading so she invited him to join a book club gathering where book enthusiasts got together and shared their favorite books. He gradually found out that it was in fact a way for them to recruit members into a strange but extremely close-knit and bonded community. As the recruitment became more and more intense and aggressive, he felt the need to leave Osaka. He came back to Chiba. Once again, he was filled with an enormous sense of failure. He could not achieve or accomplish anything in Osaka. He came back home, and it was a disappointment to himself. It did not matter where he lived, in Chiba, Tokyo or Osaka, he was a loser who was not good for anything. He was just one of his old friends who were becoming delinquents and not making any contribution to society. His life was in shambles.

Masuda felt that his life up to that point was all about running away. He ran away from his dysfunctional family. He ran away from his school. He ran away from Tokyo. Then he ran away from Osaka where he thought he could accomplish something, but he ran away again. He felt that he was not achieving anything and felt completely defeated as he was escaping from personal, professional and social obligations. He was nothing. He was nobody.

Influence from Shuji Terayama's work

Thinking back on his days in Osaka, there was one thing that influenced him and stuck with him for the rest of his life, and that was one of the books by Shuji Terayama (1935–1983), a

Japanese writer, playwright, poet and social critic that gave Masuda an enormous impact and affected his views on life and everyday philosophy. It was a light bulb moment, and something clicked in Masuda's brain when he came across Terayama's book *Sho Wo Suteyo, Machi E Deyo* (Throw Away Your Books and Rally in the Streets)[14], and to this day, he never stays inside his apartment all day, and he makes it a point to go outside every day no matter what. Once people step outside, there is always something new that they find.

He was also influenced by Terayama's style of stage performance. *Tenjo Sajiki* is one of the most well-known underground theater groups run by Terayama and his peers from the late 1960s to the mid-1970s. It was launched in 1967, and their first show was called *The Hunchback of Aomori*, and they continued to show performances with provocative titles, such as *The Crime of Fatso Oyama* in 1967, *A Mother of Eyelids* in 1968, and *Heretics* in 1971, among others. Terayama was a school dropout and a runaway kid, and his background greatly attracted a group of youths with similar backgrounds who were marginalized and dismissed from mainstream Japanese society. His performance group comprised of countercultural, avant-garde community of artists, performers, and creators. They showed their performance in West Germany, the USA, France, the Netherlands, and Yugoslavia, and became popular overseas and earned an international reputation prior to the recognition in Japan.

Terayama was extremely critical of the existing, mainstream theater performance and challenged them and conveyed messages of the antiestablishment and anti-mainstream values through his works, and this type of performance was called *Ungra* which came from "underground", and they attracted the youths, like Masuda, who were fed up and sick of the mainstream establishment at the time. From Terayama, Masuda learnt that the mold was there to be broken, and the rules were there to be challenged and violated, and that was how creativity was born. Terayama's philosophy was eye-opening for him, and he voraciously read, watched, digested and absorbed everything that Terayama had written and produced. This later led to Masuda's interests in the theater world.

Obsession with theater and stage performance

Masuda was particularly drawn to two performance groups, namely OM-2 and Self23. OM-2 was a radical theater group which was formerly called Yellow Bugidan2. Similar to Terayama's, their performance style was very unconventional and experimental and took away the boundary between the actors and the audience. They began showing their performances overseas, and had been invited to the festivals in the USA, Europe, Asia, and Africa. There were no written scripts for their performance so they were all improvised. The message was to question the reasons and meaning for living, and this was something that Masuda questioned throughout his childhood and adolescent years. He was especially attracted to their "Dancing Box" performance in which the audience was first blindfolded and taken inside a room. When the blindfold was taken off, they saw themselves squeezed into a cage with other fifty people all packed together. Then the four walls of the cage were brought down to meet the performers. This was a completely out of the ordinary theater performance. Masuda briefly had a part-time job in OM-2 as a staff, and it was years later that he realized that he had acquired the knowledge and skill to design a stage and produce a performance. Similarly, he was also a member of Self23 at Meiji University launched in 1987. Their stage performance was filled with danger, violence, and laughter, and the actors acted violently on the stage using steel pipes, chain saws, and knives. It was a life and death matter, and that was appealing to the youths who were looking for stimulation and provocation, and they were excited to see how the actors walked a fine line between life and death since nothing could be more frightening than losing one's life. Despite its deadly acts, their shows were successful. Masuda could forget about everything that was happening at home when he was participating and engaging in creative and theatrical work. He was completely absorbed in the performance groups, continued to read Terayama's work, and dreamed that someday he could direct a stage similar to his.

Encounter with Norimizu Ameya and the adoption of a new name

After he left OM-2, he met Norimizu Ameya and started assisting and working with him whom he considered one of the people that mentored and influenced him as an artist in his early twenties. Ameya is a Japanese director, stage designer, performer, and artist. His installations and performances attracted a lot of attention in the art world because they were extreme and radical to say the least, and the public rarely understood what his intentions and messages were. Working beside him got Masuda thinking about the meaning of expressing oneself through creative work. But there was no way he could earn his living doing what he wanted to do so he took a job as a back stage carpenter in the evenings for television shows. Compared to Ameya's loyal and dedicated staff who were living with him in the storage room of a trucking company, Masuda went back to his home in Matsudo which gave him a sense of guilt. He felt like a poseur, but Ameya once told Masuda, "You are not the type of person who should stay here too long." As a result, he did not. He went on with his life, but he was not running away this time.

Ameya found talent in Masuda and encouraged Masuda to write a stage script.[15] After this performance, Masuda felt the need to have a different identity and a new name for himself as an artist and performer. Sebastian is not his real birth name which he prefers not to release to the public. "I wanted a name that would be easier for people to remember so I went to a game center in Shinjuku, and there was a machine that tells you a fortune nickname if you put 100 yen (approximately US$0.67) into it and enter your birthday and some other personal information. I tried a couple of times and got two suggestions, Sebastian and Gonzales. I didn't like 'Gonzales Masuda,' so I chose Sebastian. Sebastian Masuda sounded good." He would have never dreamt that this name would be known throughout the world. This was a turning point in his life when he decided to drop his birthname that his parents gave him and adopted a new name with a new persona that offered him a fresh outlook on life.

MAMA: Masuda's performance group

His creative performance was an outlet for the repressed emotions that he was carrying all these years. He wanted to experiment and perform the modern interpretation of Terayama's work that he adored so much; he decided to launch his own art performance group and called it MAMA at the age of twenty-two while staying under Ameya's mentorship and umbrella. The main theme of the group was to pursue an innocent child's violent nature which can lead to ultimate stupidity. He had learnt from other actors and performers that excessive stupidity is art. He wanted to mix kawaii and madness, which usually do not coincide together, to generate a new concept that never existed before and provide a perspective that was genuinely fresh. His goal was to make something that evoked a lot of emotions and feelings. He recruited his friends as members who were not involved in the creative world because art-trained people had a certain frame of mind, and it was often difficult for them to get out of the fixed mindset. He wanted members who did not have any preconceived notions about what art was or what performance was.

One of the most outrageous and biggest performances of MAMA was a car that smashed into a gigantic cake with a ton of whipped cream. Both the car and the cake were crushed into pieces. Rocket fireworks were then shot into the gigantic cake, and it caught fire and created a big mess. The fire engines were called to put out the fire. It caused a huge commotion and outrage in the art community, but Masuda was so self-absorbed at the time that he was completely satisfied with the outcome and was proud of his performance believing that he was the modern day Terayama. Similarly, Masuda's art installations were also controversial. He displayed a shopping cart full of rotten sweets in colorful packages along with rotten cabbages and other trash. This was his interpretation and definition of art. He was expressing his philosophy of the cruel and dirty side of children's innocence. His slogan was "excessive stupidity is art." He wanted to make a statement that kawaii is not just a state of cuteness, and there was something more behind kawaii.

While he and his peers received a lot of attention from the art world in Japan, the feedbacks were negative and critical. No one understood Masuda's message of "childish madness" or "excessive stupidity." One of the art critics went on to write a lengthy criticism against his performance and creative display while another called him in to let him know he was a hopeless artist. He was told that if his work was ever considered art, that would be the end of the art world. Everything turned out to be disappointing, and their works were completely trashed by prominent art critics and other experts which was humiliating and painful. Masuda was more or less shunned and isolated from the Japanese art world which left him hopeless and helpless. However, this curse turned into a blessing later in his life because this was the very reason why he decided to open his shop in Harajuku where he and his friends could display whatever they wanted to. He needed to have his own space where people could stop by to see their work.

The members of MAMA were trained by Masuda to come up with strange and unique ideas. They played a card game almost every day, and those who lost the game had to think of a penalty performance, and coming up with a crazy penalty was an exercise to eventually produce an entertaining theatrical performance. For instance, one idea was to use the police station as a plot where policemen were standing. One of the MAMA members wandered around with boxing gloves in front of the police station, another passed by the policemen with his head between his hands pretending as he was punched by someone and was in pain, and the third one passed by the policemen running with a head gear in his hand which looked like he was chasing someone.[16] All of these three men secretly carried a tape recorder so that they could record the conversation between the policemen while they watched these three men passing by: "Oh,

I think someone who looks like a boxer just passed by. Was that a fight? Should we go after them and break the fight? What shall we do?" Masuda and his members later listened to the tapes and cracked up. The policemen are also human beings, and they are also sometimes lost not knowing when to take action. Masuda was reenacting Terayam's idea about finding and creating drama in one's everyday life. This was Masuda's way of performance training. He was obsessed with Terayama's philosophy about challenging the societal norms. He wanted to investigate everyday reality and how exactly it was produced and played out.

Unbeknownst to Masuda and his group members at the time, they were conducting ethnomethodology which is a sociological approach developed by Harold Garfinkel (1917–2011), an American sociologist, that studies how the process of social interactions produces social order.[17] It is one of the research methods in social sciences that investigates rules that structure people's everyday life. Ethnomethodologists often purposefully prepare a context in which social norms and common sense are challenged or conventions are disrupted to examine how people respond to the confused situation that suddenly arises. With ethnomethodology, one could explore the taken-for-granted details of everyday life and see how meanings are achieved through seemingly mundane social interaction. This methodological strategy is so fitting to someone like Masuda who wanted to provoke the audience and challenge normal situations.

The Family Breakdown

Working with Ameya took Masuda away from his family that was clearly breaking down in front of his eyes every time he went home. The Japanese economy stopped growing, was shrinking and losing momentum, and people were no longer buying expensive, luxury items, such as kimono. Masuda's family's business was hitting the rock bottom, and the father was trying out any businesses that he could put his hands on to make ends meet, and ended up carrying more debt than they already had. The father rarely came home although Masuda's mother left him a note on the dining table every night before she went to bed begging him to help out the family that was facing financial difficulties. He came home, found the note, ripped it into pieces, threw them into the bin, and left again. The mother picked up the ripped pieces and taped them together. This cycle was repeated over and over again between the father and the mother.

Masuda's distain for and contempt against his father is clear and explicit in his autobiography.[18] Having experienced Japan's unparalleled and unprecedented economic prosperity, the father drove expensive cars, wore luxury clothes, and ate and drank at expensive restaurants and pubs. Masuda remembered his father uselessly spending money like water showing off his wealth to everyone around him. The father could not change his spending behavior and stop using money when Japan's recession was clearly affecting his kimono business; he was far from a traditional Japanese father who is self-sacrificial and takes the job of protecting his wife's and children's well-being before his own. He was an irresponsible man who was indifferent to the problems that the family was facing. Masuda thought that this man was not capable of creating a normal, happy family that Masuda's mother had dreamed of having since she was a little girl. The family was in debt, rents were not paid, electricity and water bills were piling up, and the mother was carrying all the burden herself. She went into depression.

The ultimate betrayal was waiting to happen. Masuda's sister instinctually suspected that the father was having an extramarital affair with another woman, and the sister was right. The father had filed for a divorce unbeknownst to his wife by forging her signature. And there was the name of a woman whom no one knew under his wife's name in the government's family registry. When it was discovered, the father initially lied to the family explaining that he did it for money, and it was a marriage of convenience with a non-Japanese woman who wanted to stay in Japan but had no other means but to marry a Japanese citizen. However, it later became clear that he was having an affair, so he needed to divorce Masuda's wife without any legal conflict, and he also had a child with his new wife. Needless to say, the family that was already crumbling completely fell apart. Once again, the mother had a nervous breakdown and was mentally, emotionally, and physically broken.

Masuda asked himself, "How can our family go so low? We cannot be more dysfunctional than this." What is the role of a father? What is a normal and happy family? Who decides what that is? What does it mean to be happy? Why am I in this? Can I get out? How can I get out? Can anyone get out? How do you get out of all this mess? All these questions were spinning in Masuda's head, but he could not offer any convincing answers to himself. One thing he knew for sure was that he would eventually be destroyed by everyone around him, the parents, teachers, and friends, if he did not do something with his life.

Notes

1 Lunch is not provided in most of the Japanese junior and high schools. Therefore, students are required to bring their own lunch box, known as bento, which is normally prepared by their mothers.
2 Matsudo is in the northwestern part of Chiba Prefecture and is about 30–40 minutes by train to Tokyo.
3 In 1983, the Japanese yen–US dollar exchange rate was 245 yen per dollar, but by 1988, it was 128 yen per dollar. An exchange rate is an indicator of a country's financial health and economic stability. When the country's economy is strong, a currency's value goes up, and when it is weak, it goes down.
4 Sebastian Masuda, *Kakeizu Katta* (*The Family Tree Cutter*) (Kadokawa Publishing, 2011).
5 Masuda, *Kakeizu*, 2.
6 In Japan, a married couple is legally required to share the same family name, so they choose either a husband's or a wife's family name. As of 2023, in 94.5% of all marriages, a family name was changed to the husband's while 5.5% took the wife's family name. When a man marries into his wife's family and carries her family name, it is called "mukoyoushi.. Therefore, Masuda's father was married into his wife's family and was legally required to take on the wife's family name. This is often a strategy taken by families who only have daughters and no sons. It is a way to continue the family's

name since the current Japanese Constitution does not allow a couple to have different family names, and this has been much debated in the Japanese Congress.
7 Interview with the author in New York on September 26, 2024.
8 She has become a Buddhist monk.
9 Masuda, *Kakeizu*, 25–34.
10 Bessel A. Van der Kolk and Charles P. Ducey, "The Psychological Processing of Traumatic Experience: Rorschach Patterns in PTSD," *Journal of Traumatic Stress* no. 2 (1989): 259–74, https://doi.org/10.1007/BF00976231; Bessel A. Van der Kolk, "The Compulsion to Repeat the Trauma: Reenactment, Revictimization, and Masochism," *Psychiatric Clinics of North America* no. 12 (1989): 389–411.
11 Richard B. Corradi, "The Repetition Compulsion in Psychodynamic Psychotherapy," *Journal of American Academy of Psychoanalysis and Dynamic Psychiatry* no. 37 (2009):477–500, https://doi.org/10.1521/jaap.2009.37.3.477; Howard B. Levine, "The Compulsion to Repeat: An Introduction," *International Journal of Psychoanalysis* no. 101 (2020):1162–71, https://doi.org/10.1080/00207578.2020.1815541.
12 Men's suicide rates in Japan have always been higher than those of women. Since 1990, the number of men's suicides has been on the rise: 12,316 in 1990, 14,231 in 1995, 21,656 in 2000, and 22,282 in 2010, according to the Japanese Ministry of Health, Labour and Welfare. https://www.mhlw.go.jp/stf/seisakunitsuite/bunya/hukushi_kaigo/seikatsuhogo/jisatsu/jisatsu_year.html.
13 It is estimated that there are 1.46 million *hikikomori* students and adults in 2022, according to the Japanese Ministry of Health, Labour and Welfare. https://hikikomori-voice-station.mhlw.go.jp/.
14 Terayama Shuji, *Showo Suteyo, Machie Deyo* (*Throw Away Your Books and Rally in the Streets*, 1971).
15 See more details about his involvement with the art groups and his own performance group in Masuda, *Kakeizu*, 124–9.
16 See more details about his performance group in Masuda, *Kakeizu*, 127.
17 Harold Garfinkel, *Studies in Ethnomethodology* (Routledge, 1991).
18 Masuda currently has no relationship with his father.

Chapter 2

THE START OF 6%DOKIDOKI IN HARAJUKU

Not getting the kind of response he wanted from the mainstream art world in Japan turned out to be a fortunate outcome for Masuda. He decided to start a shop of his own where he could display his creative work as a self-expression. In art galleries and theaters, one's creative work is shown to the public for a limited duration, but a shop allows people to see his work repeatedly and continuously as long as they are displayed at the shop. He knew for a long time that if he was ever going to have his own shop, it was going to be in Harajuku, the neighborhood that he had spent his adolescent years in. He could not imagine having a shop anywhere else. It is the district that welcomes people from all walks of life and has a liberating atmosphere. His 6%DOKIDOKI is known today globally as a shop and a brand that represents Harajuku fashion and Japanese Kawaii culture. When the youths enter the shop, they immediately scream "kawaiiiii!" at the top of their lungs. Kawaii represented through a collage of bright, neon colors is how one sums up his world that is unique, different, and exclusive. The year 2025 commemorates the thirtieth anniversary since its first launch in 1995. But the success was not instantaneous, nor did it come easy. It was a big gamble that he took. In this chapter, I trace how the shop came about, the struggles that he went through, the success of the shop, and the recognition he has earned throughout Japan. It also addresses some of the institutional factors that contributed to the construction of the kawaii industry and subcultural communities in Harajuku, in which Masuda was one of the major players and contributors. He was in the right place at the right time.

Preparing for 6%DOKIDOKI

Masuda started looking for a space where he and his MAMA members could display their artwork; it was going to be like a long-term or near permanent exhibition space in a booth. He initially did not have any intention of making it into a commercial space. The idea was to build something similar to Andy Warhol's creative studio called "The Factory."[1] Masuda is often asked about the unique name of his shop "6%DOKIDOKI" that often makes people wonder why it is 6% and what DOKIDOKI means in Japanese. First of all, he wanted to name the shop in Japanese since many Japanese brands and retailers are in French or English, such as Fragment, Milk, Pink House, and Undercover. He explains, "I wanted to use circles, like the alphabet 'O' and zeroes. 6% has zeros and circles in a '6' and '%'. It did not have to be 6%. It could have been any number, but I thought 6% may be just the right number. I wanted to create a shop that makes your heart beat when you enter my shop, and DOKIDOKI also has 'O's.'" Dokidoki is an onomatopoeia in Japanese for a heartbeat, and it expresses one's excitement, nervousness, or anxiety.[2] The concept of the shop was "sensational lovely" and "sensational kawaii." His goal was to go beyond just cute and to achieve something that is more than cute. This is consistent with his idea about children's innocence and madness that he had attempted to express as an artist and performer.

Masuda's shop was not on the main street of Harajuku, where the American and European luxury brands and retailers are located, but in the back street that was known as *Ura-hara* where distinct youth subcultures were born. There were many so-called select shops and small boutiques where the owners' product selections were highly valued, and they became popular among the youths because of their exclusive merchandise. No two stores were the same, and each store was unique. The shops were often run and managed by young designers and artists who had just graduated from design schools or who were struggling graphic and textile designers. There were a number of collaborative projects between the shop owners and the artists that resulted in cool and trendy products. Those who shopped in *Ura-hara* were the most fashion-conscious youths, and the street style in Harajuku was a hybrid of original handmade items and popular ready-made merchandise.

6%DOKIDOKI was launched on the third floor of a building in the backstreet in 1995 with his then girlfriend and a male friend who used to work at a secondhand clothing store.[3] The monthly rent was 180,000 yen (approximately US$1,264) for a small space of 12.4 m²/133.4 ft² in size. The initial investment of 2,300,000 yen (approximately US$16,157) was split among the three; however, with the first month rent of 180,000 yen and an additional 180,000 yen for security deposit, there was not much left, so all the three owners had other jobs to support their living. Masuda managed and stayed in the shop during the day and continued to work at night as a stage carpenter, making stage sets for television shows. It was impossible to earn his living just by running the shop that was hardly making any sales. It was a struggle paying the bills for the first year.

In the beginning, they still did not have any artwork for display, so they decided to sell secondhand clothes, and one of the three owners, who used to work for the secondhand clothing store, told Masuda to go to Melrose Street in Los Angeles and buy secondhand clothes from American wholesalers. Masuda flew to Los Angeles and visited the place as he was told, but there was nothing there. He met a buyer from Japan who said that they mostly buy their products at flea markets, so Masuda visited the flea markets. Secondhand wholesalers sold old clothes by the kilos, so from the huge piles of old, worn-out clothes, he looked for sellable items and found nothing worth spending his limited budget on. He was frustrated and extremely annoyed at the friend who actually knew nothing about the secondhand business in the United States and gave Masuda the wrong information. His time in Los Angeles and money were running out, and he was physically and mentally exhausted. Then he happened to pass by a big drugstore and went in, and there he found colorful children's toys. That was when a light bulb in his head went off again just as when it went off when he first found Terayama's work during his stay in Osaka. "This is exactly what I want to display in my shop!" Then he went to other big drugstores in the area and obsessively and frantically bought all the colorful children's toys, figurines, knickknacks, gadgets, and trinkets he could find, stuffed them in his suitcases, and brought them back to Japan.

The shop was furnished with colorful walls and displayed rainbow color merchandise (Figure 2.1). However, these products initially received mixed reactions from his customers. Those who accidentally came to the shop were often flabbergasted by the gaudy colors and turned around and walked out the door. The shop was not at all commercially successful, and he remembered clearly the sales for November, 1995, one month after the opening of the shop, was only 2,000 yen (approximately US$12.70), so no wages were paid. But the three who had invested in the shop were desperate to keep it open, so they worked multiple jobs to pay the rent and running costs. Masuda borrowed money from all possible sources: family, siblings, far relatives, old friends, and "sara-kin."[4] A year after the launch, one of the three investors who did not see any future opportunities in the business quit and left the team. Now,

Figure 2.1. Masuda at the age of twenty-seven inside 6%DOKIDOKI shop (1997); Photo by Shoichi Aoki, *FRUiTS* Magazine.

it was left to Masuda and his girlfriend whose relationship later began to collapse.

6%DOKIDOKI Taking Off

Masuda's another light bulb moment was when he found the yellow T-shirts that were made for a telethon called "24-Hour Television" by Nippon Television Network[5] and sold the ones designed by a famous creator with premium. This was successful, and they sold far more than he had expected. The story was picked up by a magazine that Sofia Coppola happened to see, and she visited the shop with curiosity and mentioned 6%DOKIDOKI in her interview. And that had a big impact on the reputation and name recognition. From there, it started to roll. The number of customers visiting the shop grew every week. Masuda's skill and talent as a buyer began to shine and took off. Another hit item was My Little Pony[6] that he brought back from the United States, which was a toy collection started in 1981 and later gained a cult following. He went back and forth between Tokyo and the cities in the United States looking for attractive and charming items that can be sold at 6%DOKIDOKI. The store finally generated some profits in April, 1997, a year and half after its launch.

The unique selection of products and the creative theme of the shop, "sensational kawaii," were appealing to the youths, and it was picked up by the Japanese media frequently. Fashion students stopped by and asked him if they could sell their original clothes on consignment, and young jewelry designers who were selling their products on the streets also came by asking to sell their work in 6%DOKIDOKI. The shop provided a space for unknown and marginal labels and brands and also for designers and creators who were not part of the mainstream and wanted to remain "indie."[7] The popularity and growth of the shop were unstoppable. Masuda welcomed everyone, artists, painters, DJs, and performers, and the place gradually became a hangout place for like-minded youths who felt comfortable just being there and spending time with their peers. He was then asked to open a shop inside Shibuya Parco that was a mainstream shopping arcade in the area. With a big public exposure, it attracted celebrities from overseas, and the shop became known not only domestically but also globally. As his ambition grew, five more 6%DOKIDOKI shops were opened throughout Japan, such as in Osaka and Kyushu. However, there was only so much he could manage and control, and the theme of the shop was being compromised. The taste and message of Harajuku's kawaii culture that he strongly believed in were being lost. He decided to keep just one shop, and that is the one in Harajuku, where his philosophy of kawaii was centralized.

As the shop's reputation and popularity began to spread widely throughout Japan, Masuda's relationship with his girlfriend, whom he started 6%DOKIDOKI with, was beginning to deteriorate. He was so busy with travelling overseas, running the shop, and managing his business that he did not have any quality time to spend with her, who was mentally unstable at times and often threw tantrums. She wanted to pursue her dream to become a writer and live in the United States, so it was she who initiated the breakup, and the relationship ended. Masuda had lost two of the collaborators, whom he thought had shared the same goal with and worked together to make the business successful. He was left all by himself to run and manage the shop. Instead of feeling lonely or alone, these incidents made him even more determined and fired up to make the business successful. His ambition and enthusiasm to spread the philosophy of kawaii never diminished.

Harajuku and the Kawaii Industry

The popularity and recognition of 6%DOKIDOKI are also attributed to a number of different factors that were happening in Harajuku at that time. Masuda was in the right place, i.e., Harajuku, at the right time, in the 1990s, when the kawaii culture and industry were taking shape, and Harajuku was becoming a mecca for the youths who came looking for kawaii clothes, shoes, bags, and accessories. Street photographers were looking for young, fashionable girls and boys wearing distinct, kawaii fashion. In addition to the Lolita subculture that had a strong presence, a new subcultural community known as Decora was emerging in Harajuku, to which Masuda was making a significant contribution and was one of the key players that the followers looked up to. As explained in Chapter 1, Masuda had a special affinity and attachment to Harajuku, where he used to come every week from his hometown, Matsudo. He knew Harajuku inside and out. While the mainstream fashion cities for luxury fashion remained in New York, London, Milan, and Paris, Harajuku has carved its own position on the global fashion map. The Japanese youths play a crucial role in establishing a separate fashion community and producing the latest styles that express their subcultural affiliation and identity. Youth fashion in Japan is geographically and stylistically defined, and the kawaii aesthetic was born in Harajuku. Subcultures are defined by where they congregate, the music they listen to, the celebrities they worship and idolize, the magazines they read, and, most importantly, the way they dress.[8]

Hokoten

The roots of Harajuku's kawaii fashion date back to the late 1970s with the emergence of *Takenoko-zoku* (Bamboo Shoot Tribe), who danced in the middle of the traffic zone that was closed to traffic on Sundays so that pedestrians could walk around freely. *Hokoten*[9] meant "pedestrian paradise." There were many dance teams with flashy costumes made out of polyester satin, and they competed against each other to see who stood out the most. The more colorful they were, the more they stood out and the more popular they were. It became a part of street entertainment and attraction in Harajuku, and people came to visit Harajuku to see *Takenoko-zoku* from all over Japan. This was how Harajuku became a mecca for youths who enjoyed outrageous fashion and flamboyant self-display, which were far from mainstream, conventional fashion. *Hokoten* in Harajuku ended in 1998 because of the complaints and oppositions from the nearby residents and retailers, who found the overcrowded streets distracting. But the city never lost its vibe. By that time, Harajuku was like a catwalk where people walked down the streets and showed off their fashion, and it remained as a place where the youths congregated to meet and hang out with their friends who wanted to dress in unique styles. Therefore, *Hokoten* has a long-lasting impact on making Harajuku a place that it is today, where the youths can display and experiment their new fashion without any prejudice or discrimination from the mainstream.

FRUiTS: a street fashion magazine

No fashion is diffused locally or globally without the mass media. The production process of fashion is always strongly connected to fashion magazines. Prior to the invention of the Internet, print magazines were the most important medium to build the status and reputation of a designer or brand, spread specific fashion trends, and promote new merchandise. The diffusion process is a crucial stage between production and consumption. An object is first manufactured, and then it is transformed into fashion through the process of dissemination. In this respect, street and subcultural fashion in Harajuku has been well documented by the monthly magazine *FRUiTS*,[10] published in 1997 by photographer Shoichi Aoki, and it contained only photographs taken in Harajuku and had no text, except the captions. Aoki explained to me why he started this project[11]: "I started taking pictures of young people in Harajuku to keep a record of what is happening on the streets of Harajuku." The timing coincided with the popularity of Masuda's 6%DOKIDOKI. Aoki's goal was to report on cutting-edge street and youth fashion, and his photographs depicted a revolutionary Japanese fashion movement since the mid-1990s. The focus of *FRUiTS* was not on the designers but on the young consumers who have become the makers of street and subcultural fashion. The diverse styles shown in *FRUiTS* were continuously evolving and often unique. Aoki wrote[12]:

Because Western clothing has a short history in Japan, there is a strong tendency for people to dress in the same style as each other. Essentially this tendency has not changed. In Japan, having a different style is a kind of risk. Even the designer brand boom of the 1980s did not change that. People only took suggestions from the designers in the same manner as everyone else. Therefore, the fashion movement that came about in Harajuku was a revolution. This kind of fashion was not suggested by designers, but rather, the fashion of the young inspired the designers. On the streets of Harajuku, there was no risk in having a different style. In fact, it was considered worthwhile.

Previously, almost all print street fashion magazines published in Japan were distributed only domestically, but with the wide influence of the Internet, and through word of mouth, Japanese fashion went global. Japanese street magazines were found in bookstores outside Japan and were read by not only Japanese but also teenagers and fashion students overseas, who could not read Japanese. What used to be required to further spread Japanese subcultural fashion was a diffusion mechanism that included internationally recognized publicity and promotional vehicles, such as a fashion press, major fashion shows and events that were noticed by fashion professionals worldwide; however, all of these have become possible and were replaced by the evolving Internet and social media tools. Tokyo no longer needed the Western legitimation for youth fashion and subcultural fashion that were attracting teenagers around the world. The teenagers' radical fashion in Harajuku, with its trickling-up effect,[13] has become the inspiration for young designers.

The landmarks: Jingu Bridge, Takeshita Street, and LaForet

Harajuku has a number of landmarks where the youths visited and congregated. One of them is the Jinju Bridge, sometimes called Harajuku Bridge because it is next to Harajuku Station. The place was full of Japanese youths dressed in creative and original outfits. Some were dressed in a feminine Lolita style with lots of lace trimmings and frills around the skirt hem and on the edges of the sleeves. Others who were clearly anime and manga fans were in cosplay costumes. Decora was another subculture that emanated from Masuda's 6%DOKIDOKI where its members hung out on the bridge. This was the place where the youths met like-minded people who could share their values and norms even if they had never met each other before. They started their communication and friendship first online, and then decided to meet in Harajuku. When they met, the bond was instantaneous because their fashion was a visible indication of their subcultural membership. Another landmark is Takeshita Street, which is about 350 meter (380 yard) long and starts from a small back street in front of Harajuku Station and ends on Meiji Street, which leads to Shibuya and Omotesando, the places Masuda used to meet his peers in. The street is dangerously overcrowded on weekends, but this is the place to go to find out the latest youth fashion and subcultural fashion, such as Decora and Lolita. Youth-driven cute products are sold on this street, where small boutiques and specialized stores are located. LaForet on Meiji Street is also another landmark located in-between Harajuku and Omotesando[14] divided by the long Meiji Street. It is a shopping arcade with over a hundred boutiques and stores that sell youth fashion. The youths visit Harajuku and spend the entire day shopping, eating, and entertaining themselves, and conveniently, these landmarks are all walking distance from Masuda's 6%DOKIDOKI.

Kawaii as the Aesthetic Movement in Harajuku

A British sociologist, Angela McRobbie, explains that a youth subculture is an aesthetic movement in reference to the punk subculture as follows[15]:

There are two reasons why I have been interested in subcultures: first, because they have always appeared to me [...] as popular aesthetic movements, or "constellations" [...] and second, because in a small way they have seemed to possess the capacity to change the direction of young people's lives, or at least to sharpen their focus by confirming some felt, but as yet unexpressed intent or desire. Subcultures are aesthetic movements whose raw materials are by definition, "popular" in that they are drawn from the world of the popular mass media. It is not necessary to have an education in the *avant-garde* or to know the history of surrealism to enjoy the Sex Pistols or to recognise the influence of Vivienne Westwood's fashion. This kind of knowledge (of pop music or fashion images) is relatively easy to come by and very different from the knowledge of the high arts or the literary canon found in the academy.

Subculture is indeed an aesthetic movement, and it is also an ideological movement and phenomenon. The different styles emerging from Japanese subcultures are extremely original and creative. Those who started to don themselves in garish colors never consciously made an attempt to create a subculture with a name, but it was born organically. Similar styles mean that they share similar values, attitudes, and lifestyle, and that is enough for them to form a community because an aesthetic style is a reflection of one's mind and philosophical values. Decora now has hundreds and thousands of followers around the world, with Masuda as a central figure who spearheads the community.

The concept of kawaii

To understand Masuda's creative philosophy of kawaii, one needs to understand the Japanese perception and meaning of kawaii, which is translated as "cute" in English. Kawaii has been included in the English dictionaries for some time, along with other new Japanese terms, such as futon, e-moji, and karaoke. According to the *Oxford English Dictionary*, kawaii is an adjective which means cute, especially in a manner considered characteristic of Japanese popular culture; it is also charming, darling, and ostentatiously adorable.[16] It first appeared in the Dictionary in 2011, which shows the widespread use of the term in the English-speaking world. Similarly, the *Cambridge English Dictionary* explains that kawaii refers to the Japanese culture or style of cuteness and is the quality of being pleasant and attractive.[17] The term appeared in the *New York Times* as early as 1965 as an article heading, "When East Meets West Japanese Call It Kawaii," which was about an American designer, Helen Lee's childrenswear collection in Tokyo, and her Japanese audience at the Mitsukoshi Department store, was whispering to each other, "kawaii, kawaii."[18] Similarly, *The Wall Street Journal* published an article titled "Contemporary Kawaii Is Flourishing – There is No Japanese Word for Cloying,"[19] implying that kawaii is so cute that it becomes distasteful. No

Western writer could have ever imagined in those days that this term or concept that was uniquely Japanese would be used so widely and globally in daily English-speaking conversations.

For Masuda, "kawaii is a microcosm of Japanese culture where I can create my own closed universe."[20] It is about creating a small world within oneself. It is not just a tangible object but is a psychological and emotional state which affects one's lifestyle and views on life in general. As explained in Chapter 3, Masuda's concept is rooted in the Japanese philosophical tradition of *"hare and ke."* In the past, the special days for festivals and traditional events were referred to as *hare*, and the people enjoyed these public events by wearing elaborate clothes decorated with colorful design motifs. During Japan's modernization and westernization process, the concept of *hare* was left behind, and Masuda strongly believes that the concept of kawaii and wearing conspicuous clothes are very much related to the idea of *hare* to which he is giving a modern twist and interpretation.

The Recognition Throughout Japan

As the name of 6%DOKIDOKI began to spread throughout Japan, Masuda began to receive many invitations for projects and offers for collaborations. He instilled the concept of kawaii to apparel, food, furnishings, hotel rooms, nurseries, sculptures, art objects, and so on. He carried multiple hats and titles and was involved in a variety of fields. This was something that he had never imagined when he was struggling to run the shop in his mid-20s while losing his business collaborators along the way. He was no longer just the owner and creative director of the shop but was also a videographer, stage director, advisor to the hospitality industry, and charity organizer among many others. He has managed to juggle all these tasks with a handful of his loyal staff members, some whom have been working with Masuda for two decades.

As a fashion designer

Masuda studied fashion design at ESMOD,[21] a fashion school in Harajuku, so he understands how pattern pieces are cut and sewn together, and how textiles are printed; he used his expertise to establish a clothing line that has the same name as his shop, 6%DOKIDOKI (Figure 2.2). The fabric prints are exclusively designed by him and his product development team. His shop girls wear the brand and coordinate it with colorful accessories to create a unique style of their own. It allows a wearer to experiment different color combinations and add personal accessories to their styles. Even if two girls are wearing the same outfit, they look completely different because of their styling and coordination with different items, such as accessories, jewelry, hats, headbands, hair pins, make-up, shoes, and so on. It takes hours to pull off a fashionable Decora look, and the fans take it very seriously to create the look. Some wear plush toys on their outfit or put them on their head as a hair accessory. Masuda's brand

Figure 2.2. Shopgirls as models in 6%DOKIDOKI apparel brand (2024); Photo by Alvaro Nates, AXEL ESCALANTE.

encourages to break the mold through clothes and challenge all the conventions of how clothing should be worn because there are no rules to a Decora look or any aesthetic expressions. There were a number of clothing brands that represented kawaii at the time, such as Milk, Pink House, Angelic Pretty, and Baby the Star Bright Shine, but the 6%DOKIDOKI brand and those who wore the brand were so unique and flamboyant that they stood out from the crowd. It goes against the traditional Japanese saying "those who stood out will be hammered down." Masuda's countercultural message definitely went against the tradition. The youths felt so empowered by 6%DOKIDOKI that they did not care even if they were hammered down. Colors gave them such strength to resist and rebel against the conventional societal norms.[22]

As an artist

Masuda has created countless sculptural works and art objects and displayed them in solo and group exhibitions over the years. He has established himself as an artist, the title that the mainstream art world would have never granted him in his early 20s. He has proven to himself and to those who had given him a big stamp of disapproval that he is now an established artist.

He had a number of installations and large-scale art objects in Roppongi which is one of the major landmarks of Tokyo. In 2013, he built the Melty-Go-Round Christmas Tree that was installed at the Roppongi Hills observatory with a panoramic view of Tokyo from the fifty-second floor. The tree was decorated with colorful lights and cute items that looked as if it was melting down to the floors. He also organized another exhibition in 2017, "FOREVER COLORS" at the A/D Gallery in Roppongi Hills (Figure 2.3). It was his series of exhibitions which included Colorful Rebellion and Time After Time Capsule. In addition, the "Unforgettable Tower" was designed and installed at the Mori Art Museum for the *Sanrio Exhibition: Japan's 60 Year History of Kawaii Culture* in conjunction with the *From Hello Kitty* musical in 2021 (Figure 2.4). The tower was about eight meters high, and more than four thousand Sanrio

Figure 2.3. "A Mountain of Memories" at the FOREVER COLORS Exhibition (2019) at A/D Gallery in Roppongi; Photo courtesy of Sebastian Masuda Studio.

Figure 2.4. "Unforgettable Tower" at the 60th Anniversary SANRIO Exhibition: The Beginning of KAWAII (2021); Photo courtesy of Sebastian Masuda Studio.

character toys were glued onto the tower. In 2021, he displayed "Primal Pop" again at the A/D Gallery. More recently in 2022, "Polychromatic Skin-Gender Wall-" was installed at the Roppongi Crossing (Figure 2.5). Furthermore, he occasionally participates in group exhibitions, and he was chosen as one of the renown thirty artists and creators, such as Nara Yoshitomo, Takashi Murakami, and Mr.,[23] to participate in the "Create Your Own Original Doraemon" exhibition[24] displayed at the Mori Arts Center Gallery in Roppongi in 2017. Masuda's work was a huge three-meter high Doraemon made up of more than

Figure 2.5. "Polychromatic Skin -Gender Tower-" (2022) at the Roppongi Art Night; Photo Courtesy of Sebastian Masuda Studio.

10,000 small objects, and he titled his work as *Saigo No Uepon* (the Last Weapon). The exhibition toured to the National Museum of Singapore in 2022, the Chiang-kai Shek Memorial Hall in Taipei in 2023, and the IAG Art Museum in Shanghai in 2024.

His installations are displayed not only in major cities in Japan, such as Tokyo and Osaka, but also in the suburbs and country side. His deep respect and adoration for Terayama is widely known, and in 2016, he was given the opportunity to create a monument and exhibited his "Colorful Rebellion-the era of glitter" on Terayama Road at the Shuji Terayama Memorial Museum in Aomori, Japan. He has come a full circle to exhibit his work at the memorial museum of the artist that he so admired. His "Let's Color the Future" was installed at the Children's Anpanman Museum in Miyagi; "Dream Balloon Christmas Tree" was put up at the Terrace Mall in Matsudo, his hometown. While the themes and titles of the exhibitions and installations were different each time, the root of his message was always uniform and solid, which was the concept of kawaii represented through shockingly bright colors even to the point of feeling grotesque. His use of colors, which is his trademark, is so intense, powerful, and striking that they are immediately recognizable.

As a videographer and a stage director

Masuda was invited to collaborate with Kyary Pamyu Pamyu, a Japanese singer and model, and create her first music video titled "PONPONPON" in 2011 which had a million views in less than three weeks (Figure 2.6). Their encounter dated back to when she was still a teenager. When the kawaii culture was taking off in Harajuku, a magazine editor who was looking for a model for the cover asked Masuda if he knew anyone who had unique Harajuku-style fashion. When he asked his staff, Kyary's name came up since she was a regular customer at 6%DOKIDOKI, and his sales staff remembered her as a girl who always wore big colorful ribbons on her head with matching colorful outfits. When she was making a debut as a singer, she and her agent recommended Masuda as her videographer

Figure 2.6. Kyary Pamyu Pamyu's "PONPONPON" music video (2011); Photo courtesy of Sebastian Masuda Studio.

and creative director for her first music video. While there were some oppositions on her side since Masuda had no prior experience making music videos, she insisted that it was only Masuda who understood precisely what she wanted and could create the atmosphere that was overflowing with cuteness using colorful toys and trinkets that she had always embraced. She became a representative of the Decora subculture and Harajuku's kawaii culture and played a major role in spreading the kawaii culture with colors along with Masuda. After the success of her first music video, her collaboration with Masuda continued for other music videos, such as "Tsukematsukeru," "Candy Candy," "Fashion Monster," and "Furisodeshon."

He also art directed "Kyary Pamyu Pamuseum," a travelling exhibition that displayed the outfits she wore in the videos and onstage. Masuda always wants to surprise and entertain. He said during the shooting of her video: "If I can no longer surprise Kyary, she may no longer need me. I want to keep surprising her."[25] Similarly, Masuda has built a professional relationship with Sanrio as early as 2014 and was hired as a stage director for the recreation of "Nutcracker" as a 3D film. The original version in 1974, a stop-motion animation film shooting frame by frame with a doll, was based on E.T.A. Hoffman's original story and the Tchaikovsky ballet, and the song lyrics were coincidentally written by Terayama, Masuda's idol. Masuda was invited back again by Sanrio to direct the "From Hello Kitty" musical in 2021.

As an interior architect and packaging/culinary designer

Masuda opened Kawaii Monster Café in Harajuku in 2015. It was a café that embodied the concept of kawaii, and he designed it like a theatrical stage that entertains customers who dine there. Restaurants and cafés are not just places for eating but for having fun. At the entrance, there was Mr. Ten Thousand Chopsticks, a mascot, and the story is that he kept growing in size by devouring everything he saw and came across. The café contained elements of both cute and grotesque that he had pursued as an artist in earlier days when he was obsessed with the underground art world. There were also gigantic animal heads with huge eyes, and forks, macarons, and strawberries were hanging on the walls. There were four seating sections, each with a theme: Mushroom Disco, Milk Stand, Bar Experiment, and Mel-Tea Room (Figure 2.7). Every now and then, there was a theatrical performance inside the café, and the carousel Sweets-Go-Round placed in the middle started to spin. Masuda worked with a chef to come up with creative dishes with unique names, such as "Colorful Poison Parfait" and "Monster Burger." For Masuda, a confined space, whether it is a bedroom, retail store, or restaurant, could be used as a theatrical stage where users and customers enjoyed being there

Figure 2.7. The Melty Room at KAWAII MONSTER CAFE in Harajuku (2015); Photo courtesy of Sebastian Masuda Studio.

and were entertained. His aim was to make a spatial context that surprised the audience. It was unfortunately closed in 2021 because of the pandemic, but it is scheduled to reopen in 2025.

After the success of this project, Masuda's was known also as an interior architect and culinary designer, and the reputation spread to the hospitality industry. He was invited by Conrad Osaka Hotel in 2021 to design a sweets and deserts buffet, and he came up with a title "The Owner of a Colorful Heart." He was invited back again in 2023 for a similar project and called it "Message of Green." He also designed a sushi restaurant in New York, as explained in Chapter 3, and is currently working on another culinary project in France. Similarly, he has worked with Lotte, a South Korean confectionery company, on a number of occasions to design packages for their popular products for specific events, such as "Enjoy Halloween Kawaii" and "Enjoy Easter Kawaii." In collaboration with Tatsuma Honke Brewery Company, he designed and produced a new Japanese sake liquor called "muni" as a new product from its subsidiary brand. As an architect, he designed three newly opened nursery schools in Tokyo: "Future Tree Nursery" in Nishimagome, "Future Peace (Piece) Nursery" in Setagaya, and "Future Capsule Nursery" in Harajuku. Booking.com, an online travel agency that connects travelers with transportations and accommodations, asked him to decorate one of their rooms with a kawaii taste; he called it "Kawaii Japanese Room – Addicted to TOKYO." He also designed the window display for the "Summer Festival" at the Hankyu Department Store in Osaka.

THE START OF 6%DOKIDOKI IN HARAJUKU 55

As a participant and organizer of charity projects

Masuda has been engaging in charitable projects as early as 2007 when he started an event called Harajuku Unlimited Generation (H.U.G.) to boost the atmosphere of Harajuku that was slightly on the decline and losing its momentum, and the project theme was "to save the world with kawaii" so he decided to donate some of the proceeds to children in need of polio vaccinations in the developing and underdeveloped countries through a notable charity organization. It was rather unclear how the collected money reached the children and the overseas medical institutions so he wanted to see it with his own eyes when and how the money he and his peers donated was given to those in need. After much exploration and research on his part, he decided to join a student volunteer group that was visiting Cambodia. He was able to see a refrigerator where vaccines were stored. He took a video of his experience in Cambodia and showed it to his participants and donors at the next event when he returned to Harajuku. It was hard evidence that the money that was raised was used for these children. After this, he was officially invited by the same charity organization headed by Kayoko Hosokawa, the wife of former Japanese prime minister, Morihiro Hosokawa,[26] to visit Myanmar to see how the donated money was used. This experience taught him that one thing could lead to another like a chain. This would have never happened, had he not organized the H.U.G. project, and had he not gotten involved in charitable projects. In addition, after the earthquake and tsunami in the northern part of Japan on March 11, 2011, he launched The Mighty Harajuku Recovery Project and made Mighty Harajuku button badges, passed them out for free to people on the streets, and then uploaded pictures of Harajuku's daily life every day on social media, hoping that foreign tourists would return to Japan and Harajuku as soon as possible. More recently in 2023, he made an art object "Celebration-Ribbon" using recycled cosmetics containers for the *Charity Auction: Plastic Revives* at the Pola Museum Annex in Ginza.

Notes

1 The Factory is a work space launched by Andy Warhol (1928–1987), an American artist, in 1963 on 47th Street in New York. By 1987, there were additional three locations in Union Square, on Broadway and Madison Ave. His staff made silkscreen and lithographs, and engaged in other creative activities. They became a popular hangout place for young creators, artists, videographers and editors among others.
2 "Dokidoki" is an onomatopoeia in Japanese for a heartbeat. It expresses one's excitement, nervousness or anxiety. Onomatopoeia is the naming of a thing or action by a focal imitation of the sound associated with it.
3 Masuda, *Kakeizu*, 137–138.
4 "Sara-kin" comes from salaryman and loan. It refers to a legal or illegal money lender who makes unsecured loans at a very high interest. Some illegal lenders go beyond the legally permitted maximum interest rates.
5 The telethon "24-Hour Television" was launched in 1978 as a fundraising charity project and takes place every year in August. The aim of the program is to inform the viewers about the existing conditions of social welfare in Japan as well as around the world, and to emphasize the need for assistance towards disadvantaged people (24hrtv.or.jp).

THE START OF 6%DOKIDOKI IN HARAJUKU   57

6 My Little Pony, initially launched as My Pretty Pony, is a toy collection designed by Bonnie Zacherle, and media franchise developed by an American toy company, Hasbro.
7 Indie is an abbreviation for independent, and it refers to a type of fashion, art, film, and music, with a do-it-yourself approach and low budgets.
8 Yuniya Kawamura, *Fashioning Japanese Subcultures* (Bloomsbury 2012), 65–75.
9 Hokoten is an abbreviation of Hokosha Tengoku (Pedestrians' Paradise or Heaven).
10 Aoki's work was introduced to the international audience through the FRUiTS Exhibition in 2003 at the Powerhouse Museum in Sydney, Australia which showcased about a hundred life-size photographs of boys and girls dressed in very creative and fashionable outfits taken in Harajuku. The exhibition was based on FRUiTS, a photography book compiled by Phaidon, a British publisher. The magazine is now out of print, and it has become a collector's item among Japanese fashion enthusiasts.
11 Interviewed by the author in Tokyo on July 4, 2011.
12 Shoichi Aoki, *FRUiTS* (Phaidon 2001), 2.
13 The fundamental theory of fashion is the trickle-down theory of fashion where fashion started from the rich, upper class and slowly trickled down to the middle-class and then final to the masses. Since the late 1960s, fashion researchers have proposed the opposite direction of fashion diffusion (Blumer 1969), which is the trickle-up theory, where fashion started from the masses and is trickling-up to high fashion.
14 While Harajuku is known as a neighborhood for youth fashion, Omotesando is known as a neighborhood for luxury, high fashion, such as Christian Dior, Chanel, and Ralph Lauren among others. These two are geographically very close to each other.
15 Angela McRobbie, *Feminism and Youth Culture: From "Jackie" to "Just Seventeen"* (Macmillan 1991), xv.
16 "kawaii: adjective & noun," the *Oxford English Dictionary*, https://www.oed.com/dictionary/kawaii_adj?tl=true.

17 "kawaii: noun," the *Cambridge English Dictionary*. https://dictionary.cambridge.org/us/dictionary/english/kawaii.
18 Emerson Chapin. "When East Meets West: Japanese Call It Kawaii", *The New York Times* (April 20, 1965), 35. https://timesmachine.nytimes.com/timesmachine/1965/04/20/issue.html.
19 *The Wall Street Journal*. "Contemporary Kawaii Is Flourishing – There is No Japanese Word for Cloying" (February 21, 1986).
20 Anthony Al-Jamie. "Interview with Sebastian Masuda: Ambassador of Kawaii." *The Tokyo Journal*, 275. September 13, 2014. https://www.tokyojournal.com/sections/fashion-design/item/443-sebastian-masuda.
21 ESMOD is a fashion school based in Paris. They opened the branch in Tokyo in 1984, Osaka in 1994, and Kyoto in 2016. They train not only designers but also patternmakers. They have nineteen campuses in thirteen countries.
22 Al-Jamie, *The Tokyo Journal*.
23 Nara Yoshitomo, Takashi Murakami, and Mr. are prominent Japanese artists who are internationally known.
24 The Doraemon Exhibition, https://thedoraemontentokyo2017.jp/english.
25 "Kyary Pamyu Pamyu," Jonetsu Tairiku, a documentary program on TBS, a Japanese broadcasting company, February 27, 2012, https://www.youtube.com/watch?v=JGewNtv7HVQ.
26 Morihiro Hosokawa was Japan's Prime Minister from 1993 to 1994.

Chapter 3

EXPORTING THE KAWAII AESTHETIC FROM HARAJUKU TO THE WORLD

Masuda's reputation and the recognition of 6%DOKIDOKI were spreading far and wide. He found his creative and artistic roots in Japanese tradition and philosophy of *hare and ke*, and his message and voices, which many youths were drawn to, are heard throughout the world. His overseas activities became increasingly active. He is known as the king, ambassador, evangelist, and godfather of Harajuku kawaii fashion with international acclaim and attention. 6%DOKIDOKI has become the headquarters of the kawaii culture that is exporting their aesthetic to the world. Thanks to Harajuku, Tokyo is emerging from its history as a city of consumption, where people competed with one another to purchase expensive Western brands for status, to becoming a city of production, where some of the most innovative designers and artists in the world, like Masuda, are establishing themselves. It is also attracting attention as a city that creates a unique form of subcultural fashion. Tokyo is no longer just a city in which only Western fashion is widely appreciated and consumed; it is becoming a center that produces innovative fashion ideas in its own right.[1] While Masuda never consciously intended to establish a particular fashion subculture, Decora fashion organically emerged from 6%DOKIDOKI making the shop and Harajuku a mecca and a sacred space for the Decora fans worldwide. This chapter examines Masuda's creativity that is rooted in Japanese traditional philosophy, his international accomplishments, and contributions to Japan's soft power that uses popular culture as part of cultural diplomacy. The revival of the Decora subculture that grew out of Harajuku's distinct aesthetic style is also explored.

The Creative Roots in Traditional Japanese Philosophy

The ancient Japanese concept of *wabi-sabi* sees beauty in the process of getting older and imperfection. *Wabi* is translated as "subdued, austere beauty," while *sabi* is translated as "rustic patina."[2] This is a Japanese aesthetic uniquely rooted in tradition and history. People outside Japan often refer to subdued, earthly, and neutral colors as the Japanese colors based on this concept of *wabi-sabi* and apply them to analyze the works of the Japanese designers, such as Yohji Yamamoto and Rei Kawakubo,[3] who used black and other subdued colors in their collections and whose fashion shows take place in a quiet, somber, and dark space. This ideology is also reflected in Japanese gardens, flower arrangement, and ceramics.

Moreover, when Masuda is asked where his creative philosophy comes from, he mentions the Japanese concept of *hare and ke*[4] that was a theory introduced and developed by Kunio Yanagita (1875–1962) through his empirical research conducting ethnographical fieldwork in Iwate, Japan. Yanagita was a Japanese folklorist and ethnologist who studied rural Japan and its folk traditions and was also a founder of Japanese folklore studies called *Minzoku-gaku* as an academic field. Yanagita's theory explained the difference between special events or moments in life and daily routines in traditional Japanese life and argued that these two concepts are highly relevant to their well-being and sustainability.[5] The special *hare* events refer to extraordinary or festive occasions, such as weddings, funerals, New Year's celebrations, harvest festivals, and other exclusive events; people wear special dress and attire and participate in religious activities and spiritual rituals. On the other hand, *ke* is about the ordinary, daily, routine aspects of life, referring to the mundane chores that occur daily, such as cooking, washing dishes, cleaning the house, and going to work. In traditional Japanese society, people moved back and forth between *hare* and *ke* or treated them as a cycle in one's life; *hare* was a necessary stage in life to provide a spice to the monotonous *ke* stage, which could be physically and emotionally draining. *Hare* is spiritual and extraordinary, while *ke* is realistic and ordinary; *hare* is exclusive, while *ke* is mundane. Yanagita stated that one's life needs to balance the two to make their life stable, secure, and harmonious. Both are indispensable and important elements in Japanese culture.

Some youths today may never experience *hare* moments in life, but wearing the 6%DOKIDOKI brand literally made them feel "dokidoki" and cheered them up. It is an exciting moment in their life. As *hare* is the tradition that brings people together, the youths are bound by kawaii fashion and congregate on weekends in Harajuku almost as a ritualized activity. Masuda wanted to reinterpret *hare and ke* in his own way and treated kawaii as a practice of *hare*. One may be wearing normal clothes to work or school uniforms every day, but they wear kawaii and colorful dresses on weekends, and that is the *hare* occasion for them, bringing the extraordinary into the ordinary. This is equivalent to the twelve-layered kimono during Japan's Heian period when noble women wore the special, heavy kimono reserved for a special occasion. According to Yangita,[6] the idea of *hare and ke* was disappearing due to industrialization as Japanese in modern society no longer valued traditions, rituals, and festivals, and he could see that the mundane state of constant *ke* could lead to the weakening of cultural and spiritual fulfillment. Masuda is reclaiming the *hare* and putting it back into the Japanese society with his interpretation and introducing it to the world. Similarly, Masuda also referred to Hideyoshi Toyotomi (1537–98), a feudal lord, who introduced a special day, such as a cherry blossom viewing, known as *Hanami*, which is an example of the *hare* event because it occurs only during a specific time period in spring. In addition, the tea master, Senno Rikyu (1522–91), who introduced *wabi-sabi* and incorporated it into the tea culture, curated The Golden Tea Room, which was flamboyant and flashy. While *ke* may be closer to and associated with *wabi-sabi*, there is the other side, which is *hare*. Both are the opposite sides of the same coin or aesthetic. For Masuda, the concept of *hare and ke* is the extension of *wabi-sabi*, both of which are based on the Buddhist teaching.

Psychology and Colors

Scientists have investigated colors as early as the nineteenth century. Masuda, known as a magician of colors, pursues the socio-psychological impact of colors, bright colors in particular, on people and society, and there are some scientific explanations for his argument that colors affect one's mental state. While scientific studies on the psychology of color are still inconclusive, there are a number of academic studies that explain a correlation between one's mood and colors. In 2020, a group of researchers surveyed 4,598 people in thirty different countries on the associations with certain colors and with specific emotions.[7] Some of their findings were as follows: 51% associated black with sadness; 68% associated red with love; 52% associated yellow with joy; and 50% associated pink with love. They explained that colors and their associations with emotion can have more or less universal qualities, and colors are a part of natural and social environments, and there are both aesthetic and emotional components; human beings seem to systematically associate colors with emotions.

In addition, according to the article, "Effects of Color on Emotions,"[8] emotional reactions to color hue, saturation, and brightness were investigated using the Pleasure-Arousal-Dominance emotion model, and based on their findings, blue, blue-green, green, red-purple, purple, and purple-blue were the most pleasant hues, while yellow and green-yellow were the least pleasant. Green-yellow, blue-green, and green were the most arousing, whereas purple-blue and yellow-red were the least arousing. Green-yellow induced greater dominance than red-purple. Another similar study[9] on colors also investigated the three perceptual dimensions: hue, saturation, and brightness. The twenty-seven chromatic colors (colors beside black, white, and gray), plus three brightness-matched achromatic colors, were presented via an LED display to participants whose heart rates were measured continuously. The emotion ratings showed that saturated and bright colors were associated with higher arousal. Similarly, the hue also had a significant effect on arousal, which increased from blue and green to red. Achromatic colors (black white, and gray) resulted in a short-term decline in the heart rate, while chromatic colors caused an acceleration. The results suggest that color stimuli have effects on the emotional state of the observer, and these effects are not only determined by the hue of a color but by all three-color dimensions as well as their interactions.

While many researchers agree that the psychology of color is a new field and still lacks academic rigor, whether it is scientific or not scientific, the youths feel that their mood and personality change greatly when they are dressed in kawaii fashion in bright colors. Masuda's unwavering slogan, "Colors have the power to make people happy," is convincing to the youths who are in search of stability and optimism in their lives. Whether he is creating artwork, designing the interior décor of a restaurant and coffee shop, or making toys, his designs are always in vibrant colors and never monochromatic, neutral, or earthy colors. He believes in the power of neon colors. Masuda explains, "For example, when you change your hair color or wear a bright-colored shirt, you feel bouncy all day long." Colors can make or break one's emotions and psychological state. They are the powerful means to guide, manage, and control their feelings. The youths do not care whether it has any scientific grounding or not. They do not care whether the studies have conclusive findings or not. Colors fulfill their otherwise monotonous, boring, and occasionally tedious life that they want to escape from. They find positivity and hope in the bright, unconventional world of neon colors. The world in which they live is painted with dark and depressing colors of hatred, war, terrorism, poverty, prejudice, and discrimination. It may be simple, but bright colors lift up one's spirit and put them in a good or better mood. Bright flamboyance is on the surface, but there is a strong and important social message and psychological impact implied and hidden under the colors. The public sometimes interprets

Masuda's work as a representation of only the LGBTQAI+ community, but it goes beyond a specific community. His aim is inclusivity and diversity in the true sense of the word which consists of all genders, sexual orientations, races, ethnicities, religions, generations, and physical conditions.

The International Accomplishments

Masuda has become not only an established artist but also an entrepreneur and global event organizer. But it never came easy, and everything was always through trials and errors. He taught himself everything on the job. A fantastic opportunity arrives when one least expects it. Ever since his first trip overseas, when he was conflicted between two choices, doing it or not doing it, he always took the former, even if he was not ready for the project, overwhelmed by the opportunity, and sure to encounter obstacles and problems along the way. Through his experiences, he has learned how to solve problems by educating himself through books and by asking for advice and opinions from experts. Life constantly forces them to make decisions, sometimes big, important decisions, and they are never fully prepared for anything, so they may lose the opportunity if they wait until they are fully prepared because no one can ever be fully prepared. Take action even if it is a tiny step because it will give them a new perspective and may open another new door, and this is what motivates Masuda. All of his accomplishments come from his being a risk-taker and a challenger. That was how he built his confidence and raised his self-esteem that once hit rock bottom. They can be achieved through what they did and not through what they will or may do in the future. Masuda is showing this through his behavior and actions which speak louder than verbal words.

Masuda now has a remarkable list of international activities and accomplishments,[10] one of which is a permanent installation, "The Melty Go-Round-Harajuku Girl-" at Epcot Center, Disney World in Florida (Figure 3.1), since 2015, standing on *kare-sansui* which is a Japanese dry garden or rock garden.[11] He combined Japan's old aesthetic tradition and pop culture to construct a new hybrid. The installation recently celebrated

Figure 3.1. "Melty-Go-Round-Harajuku Girl-", a permanent installation, at the Japan Pavillion, Epcot Center, Disney World in Florida (since 2015); © Disney, All Rights Reserved.

its tenth anniversary. He is a representative and spokesperson of the Japanese kawaii culture that has been exported from Harajuku to the world.

The world tour

Someone in Paris wrote on his Myspace[12] in 2009 asking him where she could find his 6%DOKIDOKI clothes and how they could purchase them. These were the days when e-commerce was used only by selected retailers. Initially, Masuda did not know how to respond because there was no way he and his staff could fly to Paris or set up a store overseas. Then she wrote, "Why don't you bring as many clothes as you can in suitcases and fly over to Paris? We can help you sell your merchandise. You can then use the money to cover your expense." Masuda and his staff decided to take a chance; the fans of 6%DOKIDOKI in France helped find accommodation for Masuda's team, and they stayed in college dorms and churches. When the word began to spread in Europe that 6%DOKIDOKI was coming to Paris, other fans in other European countries asked him to visit them. This is how Masuda and his staff decided to go on a world tour to promote his fashion brand and the shop.

This was how Masuda and his team, which included his shopgirls at 6%DOKIDOKI, embarked on the world tour to disseminate the brand, shop, and philosophy of kawaii. They named the tour "Harajuku Kawaii Experience" when few outside Japan knew about the kawaii aesthetic or Harajuku. They also visited London and Berlin, did a fashion show and a street fashion walk, and set up a pop-up shop. Then they went to Los Angeles and San Francisco. In 2011, they planned a similar tour, adding Might Harajuku Project as a subtitle, and went to Vancouver and Seattle. The world tour was not as sophisticated and cool as it sounded. Because of their limited budget, they rented a small room, and all slept in the same room on the floor. This project was daring, adventurous, and bold, but it all paid off later in his professional career. The world tour, which consists of a fashion show, workshop, and pop-up store, continues whenever and wherever possible (Figure 3.2).

Figure 3.2. 6%DOKIDOKI Fashion Show in Toronto, Canada (2019); Photo courtesy of 6%DOKIDOKI.

The colorful rebellion and true colors exhibitions

"The Colorful Rebellion – Seventh Nightmare" was Masuda's very first solo exhibition overseas, which took place at Kianga Ellis Projects in Chelsea, New York, in 2014 (Figure 3.3). He felt that New York was the best place to showcase artwork. It was a challenging move for Masuda, but he wanted to do it because people in New York still did not know much about Harajuku, kawaii culture, or Masuda as a designer and artist. Without any external funding and sponsorship, just like his first world tour project, he paid for his own exhibition and rented a very small space on the third floor of a building for a month that could

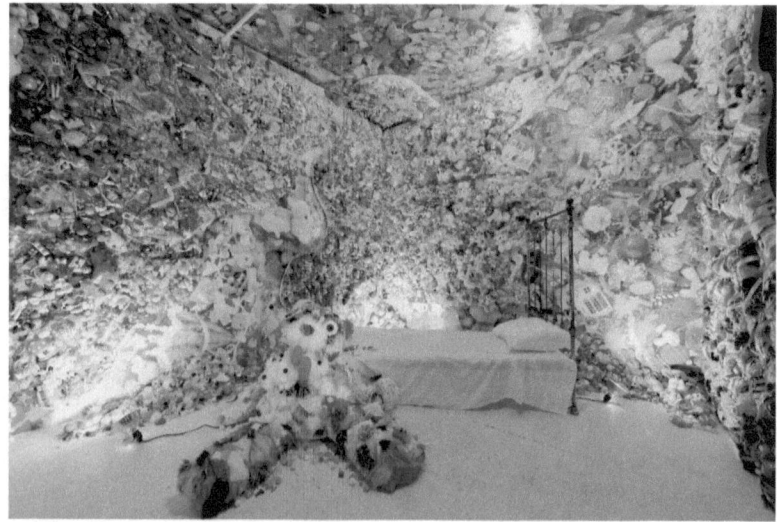

Figure 3.3. "Colorful Rebellion -Seventh Nightmare-" Exhibition (2014) in New York; Photo by GION.

hold only a handful of people. To his pleasant surprise, there were more than a thousand visitors on the opening day, many of whom were the fans of Kyary Pamyu Pamyu and Harajuku fashion who knew that Masuda was the one who directed her music videos.[13] A white bed with a gigantic teddy bear was placed in a brightly decorated room, which has become one of his trademarks. Masuda explained the Colorful Rebellion Exhibition as follows[14]:

> I have created this work as if I were writing my own autobiography. Struggling in this confined space of confession, I battle with the waves of darkness washing up against me in a night without end. I am not trying to express the grotesque through kawaii elements; rather, the essence of kawaii exists in the process by which individuals are attached to and become dependent on kawaii things. The process by which young girls become adults is full of twists and contortions, potentially resulting in a colorful mutiny. That I have created a safe haven for disobedience perhaps is my most cardinal sin. This installation only has six zones. The seventh? It's entrusted in your hands. The phrase, Colorful Rebellion, explores the possibility of inciting a revolution using the power of color in opposition to the modern world as represented by shades of black, gray, and camouflage. It originated as a title to a series of two-dimensional panels with three-dimensional motifs embedded into the surface and represented panoramic scenes from the Harajuku

neighborhood of Tokyo as well as the mental imagery of a young girl. However, for my first solo exhibition in New York, I have decided to create a self-portrait as a form and emblem of Colorful Rebellion. The subtitle, Seventh Nightmare references the Seven Deadly Sins, reflecting upon the various portal sins I have committed or to which I have fallen prey throughout my life thus far.

The subtitle of the exhibition was "Seventh Nightmare" which included greed, future, dream, fate, scar, and reality, and the seventh was a self-reflection. He borrowed the idea of the seven deadly sins from the teachings of Christianity, namely lust, gluttony, greed, sloth, wrath, envy, and price. He said to himself that introducing the kawaii culture and drawing the youths into his world may be one of the sins he had committed. If they had never come across his brand or work, they may have fit into the normal society wearing normal clothes.

Getting positive and promising responses and feedback from the American public for his first exhibition in a foreign land gave him confidence and assurance. He was invited to take the exhibition to the Young at Art Museum in Miami for two months in 2014, and in conjunction with the exhibition, he was invited by the Consulate-General of Japan in Florida to give a lecture on fashion and Harajuku culture. Then it traveled to the Padiglione Visconti in Italy in 2015. After bringing the exhibition back to the Terrada T-Art Gallery in Tokyo, it was shown at the Tropenmuseum in Amsterdam for a year between 2018 and 2019. Having been convinced that there is an audience outside Japan who is attracted to his work and message boosted his passion and enthusiasm to diffuse the philosophy of Harajuku's kawaii aesthetic, and the exhibitions helped establish and secure his solid presence internationally as a designer and artist.

Masuda returned to New York for another exhibition called "True Colors" at the Ronin Gallery in 2016 in conjunction with the Asian Contemporary Art Week. There were collages of different objects, trinkets, toys, costume jewelry, plush toys, and plastic food, all in vibrant colors. All different colors were mixed and matched with one another which represented people clashing and struggling against each other, and he saw this as a form of rebellion. In 2019, he was once again back in New York to collaborate with Special Special, a not-for-profit organization, on the "Fur East Far Tokyo" exhibition. These projects and events convinced him to relocate to New York later in his career.

Time after time capsule

The ambitious project, with the theme "Shape a Better Future for Themselves" kicked off in Miami at the Art Basel Miami Beach in 2014. Masuda distributed enormous time capsules to more than a dozen locations in different cities worldwide and invited the public to bring and fill the capsules with their personal and memorable items, objects, and written notes (Table 3.1). The capsules were in the shapes of Hello Kitty, teddy bear, and DOMO-kun, each sent to a different city. For

Table 3.1. Locations and Dates of the Time after Time Capsule Installations.

Date	Location
August 2019	The Japan Foundation, Toronto, Canada
January 2018	Japan House in São Paulo, Brazil
January 2018	Cinemateca Boliviana, La Paz, Bolivia
November 2017	Angola National School of Arts, Luanda, Republic of Angola
November 2017	V&A Waterfront, Cape Town, South Africa
October 2017	Anchorage Museum, AK, USA
May 2017	NYC, Volume 2, The Japan Day at Central Park, NY, USA
November 2016	Anime Festival Asia, Singapore
November 2016	Japanese-American National Museum, Los Angeles, CA, USA
July 2016	J-Pop Summit, San Francisco, CA, USA
July 2016	Japan Expo, Paris, France
July 2016	Camden Market North Yard, London, England
April 2016	Japan Bowl, National Cherry Blossom Festival, Washington, DC, USA
November 2015	"Hello Kitty Meets Seattle," EMP Museum, Seattle, WA, USA
August 2015	Miami Bear and Go Kawaii Go Bus, Waku Waku NYC, Brooklyn, NY, USA
May 2015	Dag Hammarskjold Plaza, NY, USA
December 2014	Art Basel Miami Beach, Miami, FL, USA

Source: sebastianmasuda.com

New York, Masuda built a nine-foot, transparent Hello Kitty capsule which was installed at Dag Hammarskjold Plaza, close to the Japan Society and the United Nations (Figure 3.4). The capsule was filled with different items and objects from the visitors, and that gave the transparent capsule colors. The more objects and items people put in, the more colorful the capsule became.

This project was very successful since it was not a one-way street project where an artist created an object and the visitors simply viewed it with admiration. It gave the public a sense of collaboration, and they felt that they were the active players personally involved in this and making the project happen with

Figure 3.4. A giant Hello Kitty statue for "Time After Time Capsule" (2015) in New York; Photo by Yusuke Sakamoto.

Masuda since the project would be incomplete without their participation and contribution. It proved to be strong evidence of how kawaii can bring people and the world together, no matter their age, gender, sexuality, religion, ethnicity, and race. The initial plan of this project was to bring back all the capsules scattered around the world to Tokyo during the 2020 Tokyo Olympics, and put all the capsules together and build a gigantic tower. Unfortunately, it had been suspended and postponed due to the pandemic.

"Yes, kawaii is art – express yourself"

This was his first solo exhibition in Los Angeles, and in addition to new objects and projects, it was also an amalgamation of the pieces he had created and displayed in the previous exhibitions and installations. He created the Kawaii Timeline as a research project in collaboration with the Kyoto University of the Arts and traced the historical origin of the kawaii culture and phenomenon in Japan. His trademark room, the "Colorful Rebellion-Seventh Nightmare," was installed in the closed corner of the exhibition space where guests could enter, lie on the bed, and take photos. Huge clock pieces from the "Colorful Rebellion-World Time Clock-" were also displayed. An interactive virtual reality project, such as *Digital Tribe World Map* and *Sense Share Bear,* which was launched for connecting and networking with the world during the pandemic was showcased. Clothes from the

6%DOKIDOKI brand were displayed on mannequins at the entrance (Figure 3.5). He writes[15]:

> It is my hope that by engaging with Japan's pop culture and the philosophy of kawaii, visitors will be encouraged to reflect on what's unique about themselves and contemplate how to navigate the social and personal challenges of the future. I would be delighted if exploring these diverse perspectives could become a hint for living into tomorrow.

Masuda's objective of the exhibition is to analyze and share his perspectives on *kawaii* while unveiling its diverse aspects.

Figure 3.5. "Yes, Kawaii Is Art-EXPRESS YOURSELF-" (2024) at Japan House Los Angeles; Photo by Kaori Suzuki.

Masuda describes *kawaii* as "a personal microcosmos of beloved things, undisturbed by anyone else." The exhibition attracted more than 10,000 attendees on the first day dressed in colorful Decora fashion, and in conjunction with the exhibition, the Free Harajuku Day in Hollywood took place at the Ovation Hollywood Courtyard with local vendors selling cute items along with Masuda's 6%DOKIDOKI pop-up shop. There were several events and programs throughout the exhibition, such as fashion shows featuring kawaii styles and a kawaii style makeover.

SushiDelic: a sushi restaurant

With the success of his Kawaii Monster Café in Harajuku in 2015, he was invited to design a sushi restaurant in New York in 2023 and called it *SushiDelic* which is a portmanteau of sushi, delicious, and psychedelic (Figure 3.6). Masuda wanted to transform the stereotypical image of a Japanese restaurant with cherry blossoms, Mt. Fuji and pagoda temples and also the conventional looks of sushi dishes. Colorful kawaii is now represented through food. The new style of a sushi restaurant created a buzz in the food industry and among the foodies, and it was featured in a number of major publications. A journalist in the *New York Times* wrote[16]:

> Enormous grinning cats dangle from the ceiling, lights look like tubes of lipstick, and a sinuous conveyor belt at a 18-seat counter delivers portions of sushi made with tuna and pink

Figure 3.6. Masuda at SUSHIDELIC in NY (2023); Photo by Naoyasu Mera.

rice on savory turquoise macarons; tempura served with a palette of bright dips; and chirashi dappled with beads of salmon roe and piled into a parfait glass. The food on the conveyor is interspersed with Mr. Masuda's playful, glittering sculptures of sushi and stilettos.

Similarly, a food critic at *Forbes* magazine wrote[17]:

It's certainly not like anything else in New York [...] his artistic visions are being realized in concert with renowned chefs [...]. The result is that the sushi and other Japanese and vegetable dishes aren't relying on their looks alone, even if your fellow, often Instagram influencers, diners are photographing every one of them under portable LED lights. They really are delicious flavors under all of that whimsy.

The interior décor had Masuda's typical bright, flamboyant color combinations, such as bright pink, purple, and blue, and there are huge cat heads hanging from the ceiling.

Everything was unique, surprising, and entertaining. It was an immediate conversation starter as customers walked inside the restaurant. There is a conveyor belt in the middle of the restaurant that circulates and brings ordered dishes and drinks.[18] Masuda was sure that *SushiDelic* in New York would be successful because 70% of the customers at his Kawaii Monster Café in Harajuku were visitors from overseas. The fun-loving nature of his designs came through in his choice of dishes and also in the interior decor. He called the restaurant "the new generation of sushi" which offers not only delicious sushi but also an entertaining atmosphere, as he did for his shop, 6%DOKIDOKI, which makes customers feel as if they were in a theme park.

Virtual kawaii tribe session during the pandemic

When the world was at a standstill during the pandemic, Masuda felt the urge and the need for his fans and followers to unite and reunite because that was when they felt most alone and lonely. He launched the Kawaii Tribe in 2020 in collaboration with the UFO (Ultra Factory Online) Team at the Kyoto University of the Arts. It was "a way to stay connected with our community – a group of like-minded people from all over the world who use the concept of Kawaii as a common language to unite them." The followers joined online from Canada, the UK, Israel, Bolivia, Mexico, America, France, South Korea, and Bahrain. It provided a space for the kawaii community and allowed them to virtually interact with one another, assuring that they were in this together, and they were not alone. In addition, Masuda posted the following mission statement titled Kawaii Tribe Speak up at the start of the pandemic[19]:

> A dark, closed world has come about in a moment.
> Not knowing where tomorrow is heading, everyone is filled with unease.
> But remember. We've been walking a path, uncertain if it was the right one.
> It seemed like a lonesome journey, but we knew it wasn't.
> We may speak different languages and live in different places, but we have all been united by our common language of "color".
> We can remember all that we've seen walking that path with our friends.
> We have the power of color.
> It is possible that we can relish the pleasure of meeting new people if we freely use our common language.

> Overcoming any possible border, such as nationality, gender, age, or religion.
> Now, although we may not be able to travel freely, let's surrender our price to the power of color.
> We can see the world using the language of color.
> Yes, let's speak up now.
> In the best way you can, before this world loses its color.
> #KawaiiTribe
> Speak Up

This mission statement struck a chord among youths around the world and was translated into multiple languages, such as Spanish, German, Portuguese, Arabic, Mandarin, French, and Romanian, among others. This was when his international network became more visible and apparent than ever as the followers came together online. Technology has transformed all aspects in societies, and the world is literally at one's fingertips and only a click away. The Internet has obviously been a major force for the growth, popularity, and spread of Japanese fashion and youth subcultures.

Contributions to Japan's Soft Power and Pop Culture

Joseph Nye (1937-), an American scholar at Harvard University, coined the term "soft power."[20] He defined soft power as the ability of a nation to achieve its objectives by attracting or seducing other nations to do its bidding or emulate its policies without resorting to coercion, which is "hard power" because gains and victories achieved by military force and economic sanctions are often short-lived and provoke a backlash.[21] Hard power does not produce any positive outcomes. Nye pointed out that it is more effective to inspire nations to adopt desired policies and objectives. Some scholars and analysts believe that Japan can use its popular culture, such as anime and manga, as soft power. Japanese popular culture has proven that Japan is able to provide high-quality cultural content that attracts millions of people around the world. Other areas of Japanese popular culture, such as fashion, music, and food, have also gained worldwide popularity. Japan is now an exporter of the kawaii aesthetic from Harajuku, thanks to a designer and creator like Masuda. It was believed that Japan lacked external cultural power, which is synonymous with a postwar strategy of constructing an exclusive and unique Japanese national identity,[22] but the Japanese government's policy has changed for the better since 2002, and it is now actively and aggressively making an effort to increase Japan's popular culture exports to help Japan's ailing economy and trade. Japanese subcultures and fashion can be used strategically as major vehicles of Japan's cultural expansion as it provides a new and alternative taste in youth fashion around the globe, just as punk fashion became an accepted legitimate taste first in the UK and later worldwide.

Japan's Cultural Envoy[23]

As the Japanese government realized that popular culture can be used as part of cultural diplomacy, they began tapping into pop culture celebrities, like Masuda and Misako Aoki.[24] In 2018, Masuda was appointed as Japan's Cultural Envoy by the Agency of Cultural Affairs and was sent to the Netherlands for a couple of months during his appointment. He stayed at Nederlandsche Dok en Scheepsbouw Maatschappij (NDSM)[25] in Amsterdam and worked on his first performance in Europe, titled "Escape From Anonymous(e)" which was reminiscent of his days in the underground theater community. This was the time when he was feeling a little lost and overwhelmed after his solo exhibition in New York in 2014, making a major debut on the international scene. He wanted to push and challenge himself and find out how much he could do. He explains his project as follows[26]:

> This project was about mice getting away from a sinking ship. I wanted to draw parallels between the social situation in Europe and the behavior of mice which can quickly notice a sinking ship and manage to escape. […] a thousand people came to watch, and we were able to put on a very large-scale performance. The kawaii culture expands when it is mixed with local elements; with this project, we were able to blend in the culture of Amsterdam and create something kawaii that was unique to the place […]. Doing this project let me

reconfirm the fact that art has the power to engage people in creativity. I decided then that I would place my faith in its power and go ahead with making art.

In addition to the government's recognition, Masuda is also well connected to the cultural and educational institutions as well as the academic world. Based on all of his remarkable accomplishments and activities, he was chosen by Newsweek Japan as one of the hundred globally respected Japanese in 2019, along with Ichiro, a Major League baseball player, and Yuzuru Hanyu, a Gold Medal Olympic ice skater.[27] He also won the New Wave Award in 2015 at the International Fantastic Film Festival in Yubari, Hokkaido; the award was given to those who were instrumental in creating a new trend and phenomenon in society. As early as 2014, he gave a lecture on Japanese kawaii culture to the students at the Middle Tennessee State University in Chattanooga, Tennessee, and the Tama Art University in Tokyo. He was also at the George Brown University in Toronto in 2019. He was a visiting scholar at New York University in 2017, studying the relationship between American youth culture and Japanese artists, and how contemporary kawaii culture was related to that. Similarly, he was appointed as a visiting professor at the Yokohama College of Art and Design and the Tokyo University of Arts and collaborated with the students on a variety of projects. In 2018, he was selected as a representative of Japan to participate in the Cultural Communication Forum in Seoul, Korea. In 2020, he was a guest speaker and gave a presentation on "The Kawaii Culture and the Global Tribal Movement during COVID" at the Color Science Association of Japan. In 2022, he was a keynote speaker at the annual meeting of the Japan Society of Kansei Engineering and gave a lecture on "Kawaii During the COVID-19 Pandemic" and was also one of the participants in the panel discussion on the impact of kawaii on the brain at the Consortium for Applied Neuroscience Symposium in Japan.

The Revival and Global Spread of the Decora Subculture

It was never Masuda's intention to create a particular subculture with a name, but it was born organically. In addition to Kyary Pamyu Pamyu whose music videos he had produced, there were other Decora influencers, such as Haruka Kurebayashi, a magazine model, and Tomoe Shinohara, a pop culture idol, who wore bright colorful fashion that originated in Harajuku in the mid- to late-1990s. Decora as a subculture began to slow down in the mid-2000s, but it is rediscovering its space and resurfacing in the center stage of Harajuku fashion (Figure 3.7). Similarly, it is regaining popularity in the US, spearheaded by a social media Decora influencer, Kristina Elle, who goes by cybrgrl; she is originally from Singapore and now lives in the US. She always dresses Decora, and her room is decorated with rainbow colors. She was very much inspired by Masuda's

Figure 3.7. Shopgirls in 6%DOKIDOKI brand (2024); Photo courtesy of 6%DOKIDOKI.

6%DOKIDOKI when she first visited Tokyo and also by Tomoe Shinohara in flamboyant clothes. She explains that accessories are a big part of the Decora style, such as hair clips, bracelets, rings, and so on. Brands do not matter, and what is important is how different items are coordinated and stylized together. She said, "Imagine if a rainbow was a human being, that would be me." She now has over 200,000 Instagram and YouTube followers. She makes it clear that Decora is not cosplay and explains on her YouTube channel that "cosplaying is dressing up like a specific character that is sourced from a variety of things, such as movies, video games and anime while people wearing Decora are not trying to be a character but they are simply trying to be themselves and they are expressing themselves through fashion."[28] The Decora subculture is now expanding as a community both in and outside Japan, and the International Decora Day, which is the last Saturday in July, has been established in 2021.

Kawaii fashion in vibrant colors is contagious and provides a positive vibe to everyone involved, not only to the people who are wearing it but also to those around them, their friends, parents, and colleagues. Decora followers donned in psychedelic colors get together at Japanese popular culture-related events, conferences, and symposia. They are also interacting with those in Japan and organizing a street walk in Harajuku with Japanese Decora influencers and enthusiasts. Although Masuda never purposely promoted his ideology of colorful kawaii to those who were going through hardships, his followers tend to be those who are known as *men-hera* who refer to those with difficult psychological issues. He understands that they had been hurt by others at one point in their lives as Masuda had, and they all share similar pain and sympathize with each other.[29]

Notes

1 Yuniya Kawamura, *Fashioning Japanese Subcultures* (Bloomsbury, 2012), 51–98.
2 "Wabi-sabi: Adjective and Noun," The Oxford English Dictionary. https://www.oed.com/dictionary/wabi-sabi_adj?tl=true.
3 Yohji Yamamoto and Rei Kawakubo made a debut together at Paris Fashion Week in 1981 and continue to show their collections every year in Paris.
4 Masuda explained this in detail at the lecture in Los Angeles in a conversation with Professor James Meraz. https://www.youtube.com/watch?v=ogmONUG7Ycs.
5 Kunio Yanagita, *Tono Monogatari* (Aozora Bunko, 1910).
6 Yangita, *Tono Monogatari*.
7 Domicele Jonauskaite, Ahmad Abu-Akel, and Christine Mohl, "Universal Patterns in Color-Emotion Associations Are Further Shaped by Linguistic and Geographic Proximity," *Psychological Science* 31, no. 10 (2020):1245–60, https://doi.org/10.1177/0956797620948810.
8 Patricia Valdez and Albert Mehrabian, "Effects of Color on Emotions," *Journal of Experimental Psychology: General* 123, no. 4 (1994):394–409, https://doi.org/10.1037/0096-3445.123.4.394.
9 Lisa Welms and Daniel Oberfeld, "Colors and Emotion: Effects of Hue, Saturation, and Brightness," *Psychological Research* 82, June 13 (2017):896–914, https://doi.org/10.1007/s00426-017-0880-8.
10 See the appendix.
11 This type of garden is often called a Zen garden.
12 Myspace, which started in 2003, was the first social networking service to reach a global audience on the Internet.
13 See Chapter 3.
14 https://sebastianmasuda.com/works/art/seventh-nightmare.
15 Japan House in Los Angeles, https://www.japanhousela.com/exhibitions/yes-kawaii-is-art-express-yourself-sebastian-masuda/.
16 Florence Fabricant, "Sushidelic Embraces Kawaii with Neon Pink Styling and Individual Sushi Bites," *New York Times*, June 20, 2023, https://www.nytimes.com/2023/06/20/dining/nyc-restaurant-news-openings.html.

17 Laurie Werner, "This Whimsical Sushi Bar is Now the Hottest Restaurant in New York," *Forbes*, June 29, 2023, https://www.forbes.com/sites/lauriewerner/2023/06/29/this-whimsical-sushi-bar-is-now-the-hottest-restaurant-in-new-york/.
18 This is known as "mawaru-sushi" or "kaiten sushi," a new style of sushi restaurant. Sushi on a conveyor belt was first started by Ganroku Sushi in Osaka as early as 1958. It democratized the sushi culture because sushi in kaiten sushi is often made by a sushi robot to expedite the process.
19 Sebastian Masuda (Source: https://sebastianmasuda.com/news/kawaiitribe/).
20 Joseph Nye, *Soft Power: The Means to Success in World Politics* (Public Affairs, 2004).
21 Nye, *Soft Power*.
22 Koichi Iwabuchi, *Recentering Globalization: Popular Culture and Japanese Transnationalism* (Duke University Press, 2002), 6–7.
23 The Agency of Cultural Affairs appointed several cultural envoys and sent them overseas to introduce and promote Japanese culture and traditions. It started in 2003 and ended in 2020.
24 Misako Aoki was appointed as a Kawaii Ambassador in 2009 by the Japanese Ministry of Foreign Affairs.
25 NDSM is a neighborhood in Amsterdam where a shipbuilding company was located. It became a neighborhood for the poor, but then it was gentrified in 2000 and has become a community for galleries and spaces used for performances and other creative activities.
26 Mizushima, *Roppongi Mirai Kaigi*. https://6mirai.tokyo-midtown.com/en/interview/97/.
27 Newsweek Japan, "The Hundred Most Respected Japanese in the World," 2019: April 30–May 7th Issue.
28 Cybr.grl, YouTube, https://www.youtube.com/c/cybrgrl.
29 Interview with the author in NY on September 26, 2024.

Chapter 4
A NEW CHAPTER IN NEW YORK AND BEYOND

Masuda has built his professional career a little by little and one step at a time while overcoming many obstacles along the way both in his personal and professional life, but he continues to act, move, grow, challenge, and never maintains the status quo. Even during the pandemic which was a challenging time for everyone, and it was almost normal for anyone to take a step back and regress in life, Masuda never stopped. He kept on going and figured out ways to connect and reconnect with his dedicated followers and fans who spread and repeated his slogan "Color the World" hoping to bring peace to the world with his trademark neon colors and kawaii images. He is determined to disseminate Japan's kawaii culture and has been making an attempt to transcend the national boundaries and identities while getting rid of the geographical confines of Japan. Keep walking. Keep moving. Don't stop. If you stop, nothing will change, and the world will then come to a halt. Nothing will change if you stop. Just take a small step at a time. He is an epitome of someone who spreads positivity in life which is contagious, and has become a role model to the youths. He has definitely proved those who had criticized and did not approve of his creative work in the past wrong. He has shown to the world that one does not need a language to communicate because they can communicate through colors which serve as a non-verbal communication tool. His ambition, enthusiasm, and determination have been further accelerated and intensified, and he has decided to relocate to New York.

Another Creative Base in New York

Having travelled to different cities in the world and experienced a variety of diverse cultures, it was his longtime dream to live abroad and have another creative base somewhere outside of Japan. Ever since his first show in Chelsea, NY in 2014,[1] Masuda had been planning to relocate to New York for quite a while, and when he was finally ready to make a move, the pandemic hit so it was delayed for a couple of years, but that did not discourage him from the relocation. He waited. He wrote in his blog titled "Viva la Vida"[2] on the day of his departure to New York:[3]

> I am moving my base to New York! […] It took three years of preparation, and I finally have my visa. I am already over

fifty, and if I want to do something challenging, I might as well do it now while I am physically and emotionally capable of doing it [...]. I am so grateful to my staff who believe in me.

He arrived in New York in February 2022. He has come far and a full circle; New York is a city that has a special place in his heart. A few weeks after his arrival in New York, he wrote again in his blog:[4]

> It's been about twenty days since I arrived in New York. I feel like the city has opened up. I'm excited! [...] I was feeling down for the first three days and really wanted to go back. But I am now getting used to a lifestyle here, and things are starting to move in a positive direction. I am determined to start everything from a scratch in New York [...] I am a newcomer here so going to a laundromat and doing grocery shopping are fun."

New York is known as the city that never sleeps. It has so much energy and power that one could get lost, stepped on, and get hurt anytime literally and figuratively. It is one of the most ethnically and racially diverse cities in the world where people from different countries and cultures intersect which could also result in conflict and misunderstanding. It is not easy to be a newcomer to the city. If one is a tourist staying in New York for a couple of days or weeks, one would probably see only the positive and fun side of the city, watching a Broadway musical, shopping at Saks Fifth Ave and Tiffany's, going up the Empire State Building and so on. But if they decide to work and live there, it gives them a totally different perspective. There are crimes, prejudice, discrimination, hostility, and many other hardships that visitors do not see or experience.

Unlike some of the Japanese celebrities who had recently relocated to New York from Japan with their staff members, assistants, and managers, and rented a room in a high-rise apartment in an upscale neighborhood of New York, Masuda had done it all alone and all by himself which he is extremely proud of (Figure 4.1). It built his confidence and the ability to overcome obstacles and solve problems in the challenging environment which he had been doing all his life. Something as simple as renting an apartment was difficult for Masuda; he was unable to find a landlord who would rent him a room because he did not have any credit history in the US. After some search and trials, he was fortunate to meet a landlord who had a good experience renting his apartment to a Japanese tenant who never missed their monthly payment, and Masuda was able to rent an apartment in a not-so-safe neighborhood in Manhattan which he "would not recommend to women".[5]

Once Masuda settled in his new apartment, there was a water leak in his bathroom, which was going to an apartment below him, and he had to make an urgent phone call to his landlord and explain the situation in his limited English. This is a nightmare that all New Yorkers go through since the

Figure 4.1. Masuda Strolling in Lower East Side, NY (2023); Photo courtesy of Sebastian Masuda Studio.

buildings in New York are very old, and plumbing issues are an everyday occurrence. Similarly, getting an undelivered package redelivered by phone was another headache and challenge for Masuda. He called all these incidents are a part of "New York Baptism." These incidents are unavoidable for long-term residents and are prerequisites before you become a real New Yorker. This is how New York welcomes newcomers!

Masuda who had been questioning the definition of what is normal since childhood and ended up doing things that are not normal by the Japanese standard throughout his adult life is once again doing something not normal. It is unconventional for Japanese men in their 50s to remain single and have no children. It is not normal or conventional for them to relocate and move the base to a foreign country and start everything anew. That is when "normal" people start planning their "normal" retirement or have already retired. Masuda is not retiring but far from it. This is a new chapter in his life. Doing something not normal allows people to accomplish things that other people would have never accomplished although there was never a guarantee that they would achieve anything outstanding. That is the risk that Masuda took and has been taking. He is willing to push himself for another ten years until his 60s:[6]

> I feel that everything that I had gone through became the solid foundation of what I do now and made me who I am today. Nothing is a waste in life. Even the most difficult times that one goes through can turn out to be a positive experience in the future although you are not aware of it when you are going through the tough times. Because of my hearing impairment as a kid, my visual sensitivity was honed. When you have some sort of physical sensory restrictions or limitations, it sharpens your other senses. But no one in my family ever looked at it in that way.

Everything in life is relative, and everything in life depends on a perspective. If one wishes to look at an incident from a negative perspective, it is a negative outcome. If one wants to take a positive viewpoint, it is a positive outlook. People decide their reality which is socially constructed and can interpret it in any way they choose to.

His Future Goals in NY and Beyond

One of his plans in New York is to set up a space where young artists and creators from different parts of the world can come together and work on their creative projects. Today's youths communicate and interact heavily and constantly online, but Masuda feels that it is completely different from the direct, face-to-face interactions where people meet each other, feel their physical presence and look each other in the eye. In addition, he explains why he moved to New York:[7]

> [...] the foremost reason is that when doing art activities in Japan, the scale of my works tends to get small, and I wanted to avoid that. I don't like the fact that the scale of my works is being constrained by factors such as budget issues and clients' requests. I want to directly transform the ideas in my mind into reality. I want to make the scale of my works bigger. My desire became stronger and I decided to move my place of work abroad.

Masuda now spends almost half of a year outside of New York, traveling the world, giving lectures, having exhibitions, attending events, and setting up pop-up stores. He aggressively and enthusiastically engages in creative activities in New York and elsewhere. His ambition is unstoppable. He went back and forth between New York, Tokyo, and other parts of the world in 2024. The first exhibition since his relocation to New York was the COLORS FOR PEACE charity exhibition at the Mizuma and Kips art gallery in 2022 (Figures 4.2 and 4.3), and the profits from the works sold are donated to the Ukrainian National Women's League of America and the human rights organization that support Ukraine. The event was supported by the Consulate-General of Japan in

Figure 4.2. Masuda preparing for the COLORS FOR PEACE Exhibition in NY (2023); Photo courtesy of Sebastian Masuda Studio.

Figure 4.3. Masuda with his followers in Decora fashion at the COLORS FOR PEACE Exhibition reception in NY (2023); Photo by GION.

New York promoting world peace while creating a safe society where people can sleep in their beds every night. He writes: "The theme of the event is seemingly simple: think peace. But please close your eyes and imagine it. And then, please realize how comforting it is to peacefully sleep in your own bed at home tonight."

In addition to his first solo exhibition in Los Angeles and the launch of a sushi restaurant, *Sushidelic*, in Chelsea,[8] NY, he was invited by the Asian Studies Student Research Group at the SWPA University in Poland and gave a lecture on Japanese pop culture in the twenty-first century kawaii fashion and Harajuku;

he was a guest DJ at the Holiday Matsuri in Florida; he attended the Cali International Book Fair in Colombia to give a lecture and workshop. His Doraemon statue, "The Last Weapon," as part of the Doraemon Exhibition which started in Tokyo in 2017, travelled to Singapore; his "Unforgettable Tower" is installed at the entrance of the Iwate Museum of Art as part of the Sanrio Exhibition: 60 Years of Kawaii Culture which is touring through Japan; he was an advisor for the "FUKUSHIMA KAWAII KOGEI" project which displayed their arts and crafts items, such as chopsticks, plates and toys, at the Japan Expo in Paris in the summer; the year 2024 ended with the Kawaii Holiday event in NY which he collaborated with TEN TEN nyc, a not-for-profit organization and gave a workshop on teddy bears.

As expected, Masuda's schedule was full of projects and activities as his international recognition spreads. Having been in New York as a resident for three years, he sees some parts of the city that tourists do not see[9]:

> I used to go to Soho and Greenwich Village when I was a visitor, but I never took a trip to Harlem or East Harlem. I see there are many social problems in this city, like shooting and drug dealing. I think there is a role that my colors can play here. There is something that I can do as an artist. In NY, when people want solace or comfort, they go into drugs, and to make money, they go into drug dealing. I thought there is a room for colorful kawaii which is comforting.

His creativity and colors may heal some of the psychological pains and struggles that people are going through in New York. There are infinite possibilities and opportunities in New York that he sees.

Colorful Kawaii as Empowerment

As early as 2008, Masuda knew that psychedelic colors and kawaii have the power to heal. He was watching a news segment on TV about a big natural disaster in Sichuan, China which killed more than 70,000 people. The damage was especially bad near a school, and while many in the area were still recovering from the unimaginable nightmare of getting their homes destroyed and facing their loved ones' deaths, school supplies, pencil cases, pens, and erasers, with colorful anime and manga characters were donated by corporations to the school children. When these items were handed out to the students, their faces suddenly lit up with excitement and joy, and they had beaming smiles.[10] That was indeed the *"hare"* moment that Masuda always had in mind.[11] It provided a small but colorful and kawaii moment and experience to the cruel reality of life. Colors are powerful, effective, and therapeutic. He explained:[12]

> The word *kawaii* works as an adhesive between our vast contemporary culture, […] It unites objects, fashion, and art from seemingly totally different genres. From Hello Kitty, to lunch boxes, to Harajuku fashion, all are

connected by *kawaii* [...] close to the spirit of the punk and the hippie, representing the fashion of rebellion against the present state of society.

Kawaii fashion for adults is sometimes criticized and ridiculed as childish and infantile, but more and more grown-up girls and women in Europe and the USA are getting attracted to the style. Caucasian women are expected to mature quickly and looking feminine in a sexual way is valued and encouraged. However, kawaii fashion offers them an alternative definition of beauty and femininity that does not show their body shapes or skin. In Decora fashion, the attention is focused on their bright colors which lift up one's mood. Girls and young women all over the world relate to the style. They are free to experiment any style in Harajuku which is a city that embraces originality and uniqueness in fashion and art. It has a very liberal atmosphere and environment. Kawaii fashion is changing the perception of what a strong woman looks like. Decora is like an armor that makes them feel strong and empowered, and it changes a wearer's personality.

Since creating the Harajuku-based kawaii fashion outlet 6%DOKIDOKI in 1995, Masuda has worked relentlessly to spread Harajuku culture to people all over the world. His unyielding passion to color the world has not limits. He explained:[13]

> If their position in society or in their community is raised because of the colorful cute dress that they wear, that

really makes me happy. There is like a school caste where you are a leader of a group while others are left out in the lower end of the strata. But because of their dress, they step up to a higher position […] Art and fashion can make what you want to say visible. For the next 10 years, I plan to visualize the messages in a creative shape and form.

The global popularity of Masuda's kawaii philosophy has grown bigger than he had ever imagined to be. Future has no limitation and is full of possibilities, and he is an inspiration to those who have big dreams to achieve.

Notes

1 See Chapter 3.
2 It means "long live life" in Spanish.
3 Sebastian Masuda-My NY Diary: Viva La Vida https://note.com/sebastea/n/n7817ecdee5e8.
4 Sebastian Masuda-My NY Diary: I am still a newcomer. https://note.com/sebastea/n/n99b965b33522.
5 Interview with the author in NY on April 8, 2025.
6 Interview with the author in NY on April 8, 2025.
7 Mizushima, interview.
8 See Chapter 3.
9 Interview with the author in NY on September 26, 2024.
10 Masuda, *Sekai ni*, 38–40.
11 See Chapter 4.
12 "Sebastian Masuda Forments a Kawaii Rebellion at Ronin Gallery", Ronin Gallery, posted on October 28, 2016. https://www.artsy.net/article/artsy-sebastian-masuda-foments-a-kawaii-rebellion-at-ronin-gallery-in-new-york.
13 Interview with the author in NY on September 26, 2024.

CONCLUSION: PAINTING AND ENERGIZING THE KAWAII WORLD WITH COLORS

6%DOKIDOKI has become a shop where foreign celebrities stop by when they visit Harajuku. Sofia Coppola once visited his shop and mentioned it in an interview, and the words began to spread, and other stars, such as Lady Gaga, Aliana Grande, Niki Minaj, and Katy Perry have also visited the shop. Life is unpredictable with full of uncertainties so one can never be fully prepared for anything that may occur in their later life. One never knows where their path is directed to. One thing leads to another, and their initial intentions and goals may change unexpectedly for the better or worse. One needs flexibility to adjust to these unexpected events, and that was exactly what Masuda has been doing.

Because of his hearing difficulty, Masuda's ability to visually take in colors was strong and sensitive, and his childhood experience of spending time in the shopping arcade in his hometown and buying trinkets in colorful packages stayed in his memory until it creeped up when he got involved in the art world. He was naturally drawn to bright colors because there was a sense of nostalgia. Furthermore, because he was always hanging out in Harajuku, it had a special place in his heart. It was the community that taught him how to be an adult and to find out that some people might not be able to make anything out of life while others chose to move on in search of a better and more constructive life. Masuda has centralized his colorful kawaii culture in Harajuku knowing all the positive and negative aspects of the neighborhood. Tokyo in the 1970s and 1980s was not the place where trends were created, but that presumption has changed over the years. Tokyo, Harajuku in particular, has become a city that produces creative and new styles because the youths continue to experiment them. It is becoming a true fashion force thanks to designers and artists like Masuda who has made Harajuku their headquarters and creative base.

In addition, his empty and lonely days in Osaka turned out to be fruitful because of his discovery of Shuji Terayama's work which he recommends to all youths. If his application to the art school in Osaka was accepted, he would have been busy going to school and would have never visited the local library every day, and he would have never discovered Terayama whom he adores and respects. His obsession with the underground art and theater world was meaningful and beneficial because that was where Masuda found his lifelong theme of children's innocence, cruelty, and madness, all combined in one. His

CONCLUSION

creative work is not all cute but is a hybrid of cuteness and some scary and grotesque elements, such as gigantic cat heads with ominous eyes hanging from the ceilings or a huge white mouse placed on the wall. Because he could not earn his living being an artist in the underground art community, he worked as a stage carpenter for television in the evening. He learnt how to draw an architectural draft which was a skill that could be used for designing a stage set or a room. It allowed him to take on architectural projects later in his career.

Moreover, not getting any positive feedback from the art community forced Masuda to open his own shop. If his creative work was appreciated and approved by the mainstream art world, and if he had received offers from major art galleries to exhibit his work, he would not have opened his shop. 6%DOKIDOKI would have never existed. He flew to Los Angeles looking for second hand clothes that could be sold at the shop but did not find anything. If he did, he might have never walked around the city and went inside the drugstore to find colorful toys and trinkets. His shop would have been like any other secondhand clothing store in Harajuku. All of these experiences provided him with a foundation and prepared him to soar to the international stage as a designer and creator. With all the skills, knowledge, and talent that he had acquired throughout his life, he is ready to paint and energize the kawaii world with colors and to bring peace to people's lives. He is who he is today because of everything he had experienced and gone through. He is a man of persistence, resilience, and tenacity.

APPENDIX A

Sebastian Masuda's Major International and Domestic Projects and Activities (1995–2025)

Year	Location	Title	Genre
2025	New York, USA	Kawaii Holiday Market: Kawaii Tote Bag Workshop	Event
2025	Kyoto, Japan	"FUTURE TRAIN," a restaurant inside the old Thunderbird express train operated by the West Japan Railroad Company	Art direction
2024	New York, USA	Kawaii Holiday Market: Teddy Bear Workshop	Event
2024	Cali, Colombia	Cali International Book Fair	Event
2024	Warsaw, Poland	"Japanese pop culture in the 21st century: Kawaii fashion and Harajuku subculture" at the Asian Studies Student Research Group, SWPS University	Lecture
2024	Chiba, Japan	"Primal POP-PPC-" at MIFUNEYAMA COFFEE, Kisarazu Station	Permanent installation

(Continued)

Year	Location	Title	Genre
2024	Shanghai, China	"The Last Weapon" at the Doraemon Exhibition Shanghai 2024	Exhibition
2024	Iwate, Japan	"Unforgettable Tower" at the Sanrio Exhibition: 60 Years of Kawaii Culture in Iwate	Exhibition
2024	Paris, France	"FUKUSHIMA KAWAII KOGEI" at the Japan Expo Paris	Design project
2024	Los Angeles, USA	"Exploring Japanese Colors with Sebastian Masuda" in conversation with Prof. James Meraz of Art Center College of Design	Lecture
2024	Los Angeles, USA	"Yes, KAWAII is Art—EXPRESS YOURSELF-" at Japan House	Exhibition
2023	Osaka, Japan	"Message of Green-Happy Holidays-" Christmas Tree and Sweets Buffet at Conrad Osaka	Installation and project
2023	Japan	"Charlie and the Chocolate Factory," a Japanese version of the Broadway musical	Art direction
2023	New York, USA	"SushiDelic," a sushi restaurant	Art direction
2023	Osaka, Japan	"Polychromatic Skin – Gender Wall" at Parc Kitagawa	Permanent installation
2023	Toyama, Japan	"Polychromatic Skin – Gender Tower #Hokuriku-" at GO FOR KOGEI 2023	Exhibition

(Continued)

APPENDIX A

Year	Location	Title	Genre
2022	Ishimaki, Japan	"Microcosmos-Melody-" Piano	Installation
2022	Tokyo, Japan	"Polychromatic Skin – Gender Tower-" and "Polychromatic Skin – Gender Wall-" at the Roppongi Art Night 2022	Installation
2022	Osaka, Japan	"Polychromatic Skin Osaka"	Installation
2022	New York, USA	"COLORS FOR PEACE" at Japan Foundation	Exhibition
2022	Miyagi, Japan	"Let's Color the Future" at Anpanman Children's Museum	Installation and project
2021	Tokyo, Japan	"Yes, Kawaii is Art" at the Kanda Myojin Shrine	Exhibition
2021	Tokyo Japan	"Primal Pop" at A/D Gallery, Roppongi Hills	Exhibition
2021	Tokyo, Japan	"Future Capsule Nursery School" in Harajuku	Design project
2021	Tokyo, Japan	"From Hello Kitty," a Sanrio musical	Stage and art direction
2021	Osaka, Japan	"Owner of a Colorful Heart," a sweets buffet, and a decorated room at Conrad Osaka Hotel	Art direction and project
2021	Tokyo, Japan	"Primal Pop (Pac Man Mix)" in the lobby of Bandai Namco Research Center	Permanent installation

(Continued)

Year	Location	Title	Genre
2021	Osaka, Japan	"Yes, Kawaii is Art"	Exhibition
2021	Tokyo, Japan	"Unforgettable Tower" at the 60th Anniversary SANRIO Exhibition: The Beginning of KAWAII	Installation
2021	Chiba, Japan	"Microcosmos – Thank You All-," a decorated piano at Kisarazu Station	Installation
2021	Kyoto, Japan	"Discovering the Digital Tribe through Kawaii" with the students at the Kyoto University of the Arts	Exhibition
2021	Tokyo, Japan	"Fantastic Voyage" at BUoY Art Center in Kitasenju	Installation
2020	Tokyo, Japan	"KAWAII Culture and the Global Kawaii Tribe Movement during COVID," at the Color Science Association of Japan	Lecture
2020	Japan	"KAWAII Company" brand in collaboration with Felissimo, a company that sells lifestyle products online	Design project
2020	Tokyo, Japan	"Pointrythm World-Message-of-Green-" at the Christmas Smile Exhibition, Pola Museum	Charity exhibition
2020	Texas, USA	"Paint It Colorful" at Japan-America Society, Houston	Lecture

(Continued)

APPENDIX A

Year	Location	Title	Genre
2020	Tokyo, Japan	"Future Tree Nursery" in Nishimagome	Design project
2019	Chiba, Japan	"Dream Balloon Christmas Tree" at Terrace Mall, Matsudo	Installation
2019	Japan	"Kawaii Japanese room – Addicted to TOKYO" in collaboration with Booking.com	Design project
2019	Japan	"Artists Collection by Sebastian Masuda" featuring Toy Story in collaboration with Disney's stores	Design project
2019	Tokyo, Japan	"Forever Colors" at A/D Gallery, Roppongi	Exhibition
2019	Toronto, Canada	Time After Time Capsule, at The Japan Foundation	Installation
2019	Tokyo, Japan	"Sebastian Masuda ART Bear" at DELL Design Labo, Omotensando Hills	Installation
2019	Tokyo, Japan	"Future Piece (Peace) Nursery"	Design project
2019	Japan	"Yoshi's Crafted World for Nintendo Switch," a TV commercial	Art direction
2019	Japan	Designed a logo and uniform for the soccer team "Asian Eleven"	Design project

(Continued)

Year	Location	Title	Genre
2018	New Yor, USA	"Fur East Far Tokyo" at Special Special	Exhibition
2018	Amsterdam, the Netherlands	"Colorful Rebellion" at the Troppenmuseum	Exhibition
2018	Japan	Designed Japanese sake liquer, "muni" in collaboration with Tatsuma Honke Brewery.	Design project
2018	Osaka, Japan	"New Generation Plant #2-Mushroom-" at Tsutaya, a book store, in Nakazakicho	Installation
2018	Seoul, Korea	Cultural Communication Forum as Japan's representative	Lecture
2018	Osaka, Japan	"Summer Festival" window display at the Umeda Hankyu Department	Art direction
2018	Japan	Lotte "Enjoy Halloween" and "Enjoy Easter Kawaii" packaging design in collaboration with Lotte	Design project
2018	Tokyo, Japan	"Microcosmos-Melody-" at the Art Piano in Marunouchi	Installation
2018	Tokyo, Japan	"Mokushi Robot" in collaboration with Angolmois, the Monster Strike Exhibition	Installation
2018	Sao Paolo, Brazil	"Time After Time Capsule" at Japan House in Brazil	Installation

(Continued)

APPENDIX A

Year	Location	Title	Genre
2018	La Paz, Bolivia	"Time After Time Capsule" at Cinemateca Boliviana	Installation
2017	Japan	"Freshlight" hair dye package design	Design project
2017	Amsterdam, the Netherlands	Cultural Envoy by the Japanese Agency of Cultural Affairs	Appointment
2017	Tokyo, Japan	"Point Rhythm World – Monet's Microcosm-" at Pola Museum Annex	Exhibition
2017	Tokyo, Japan	"Your Colors" Exhibition at the A/D Gallery in Roppongi	Exhibition
2017	Luanda, Republic of Angola	"Time After Time Capsule" at Angola National School of Arts	Installation
2017	Cape Town, South Africa	"Time After Time Capsule" at V&A Water Front	Installation
2017	Alaska, USA	"Time After Time Capsule" at The Art of Fandom, Anchorage Museum	Installation
2017	New York, USA	"Time After Time Capsule NYC, Volume 2" at The Japan Day in Central Park	Installation
2017	Tokyo, Japan	"10,000 yen Art – 3/100 Teddy Bear" Exhibition at Sezon Art Gallery	Exhibition
2017	Tokyo, Japan	"Noise Is Colorful" 6-D Sebastian Masuda 1st Fashion Show	Fashion show

(Continued)

Year	Location	Title	Genre
2016	Tokyo, Japan	LalaPort Halloween Week	Art direction
2016	Aomori, Japan	"Color Rebellion—the era of glitter" on Terayama Road	Installation
2016	New York, USA	"TRUE COLORS" Exhibition, at Ronin Gallery	Exhibition
2016	Singapore	"Time After Time Capsule" at Anime Festival Asia	Installation
2016	Los Angeles, USA	"Time After Time Capsule" at the Japanese-American National Museum	Installation
2016	San Francisco, USA	"Time After Time Capsule" at the J-Pop Summit	Installation
2016	Paris, France	"Time After Time Capsule" at the Japan Expo	Installation
2016	London, England	"Time After Time Capsule" at the Camden Market North Yard	Installation
2016	Washington DC, USA	"Time After Time Capsule" at the National Cherry Blossom Festival	Installation
2016	Tokyo, Japan	"Acchi to Kocchi: Knockin' on Heaven's Door" Exhibition	Exhibition
2016	Hokkaido, Japan	Baseball uniform design in collaboration with the Nippon Ham Fighters for the FIGHTERS FOR GIRLS DAY Project.	Design project

(*Continued*)

APPENDIX A

Year	Location	Title	Genre
2015	Osaka, Japan	"New Generation Plant" in collaboration with the Ultra Factory of Kyoto University of Arts at Kagaya Forest	Permanent installation
2015-	Orlando, Florida	"Melty-Go-Round-Harajuku Girl-" at the Japan Pavilion, Epcot Center, the Walt Disney World	Permanent installation
2015	Tokyo	Kawaii Monster Café	Restaurant
2015	Tokyo, Japan	Participation in the "Miracle Gift Parade" at Sanrio Puroland	Event
2015	Tokyo, Japan	"TRUE COLORS" exhibition in Roppongi	Exhibition
2015	Aichi, Japan	"Day Dream" Christmas Tree at Asunal Kanayama	Installation
2015	Tokyo, Japan	Renewal of a morning show set for "PON" at Nippon TV	Stage design
2015	Japan	Package design for "Body Shop" products for the 25th Anniversary of Japan launch	Design project
2015	Tokyo, Japan	"SEIBU HALLOWEEN 2015 in Nerima" in collaboration with Seibu Railway	Art direction
2015	Japan	"The Love Letters" a book by Shuji Terayama	Art direction

(*Continued*)

Year	Location	Title	Genre
2015	Japan	Package design for Baumkuchen (Tree Cake) in collaboration with Taneya Group, a Japanese confectionary maker	Design project
2015	Milan, Italy	"Able and Partners Tokyo Design Week in Milan 2015"	Art direction
2015	Japan and the Netherlands	Participation in "Miffy Art Parade" as part of the Miffy Exhibition for the 60th Anniversary event	Event
2015	Japan	Costume design for a TV commercial for "Hebel House," a building material company	Design project
2015	Seattle, USA	Time After Time Capsule "Hello Kitty Meets Seattle" at the EMP Museum	Installation
2015	New York, USA	Time After Time Capsule Miami Bear and Go Kawaii Go Bus at Waku Waku NYC, Brooklyn, USA	Installation
2015	New York, USA	Time After Time Capsule at the Dag Hammarskjold Plaza	Installation
2015-	FL, USA	"Melty-Go-Round–Harajuku Girl-" at the Japan Pavilion, Epcot Center, Disney World in Florida	Permanent installation

(Continued)

APPENDIX A

Year	Location	Title	Genre
2014	Tokyo, Japan	"Moshi Moshi Box" at the Tourist Information Office in Harajuku	Installation
2014	Tokyo, Japan	"Lumine Asobi," the New Year Project in collaboration with Lumine and Asobi System	Art direction
2014	Miami, USA	Time After Time Capsule at the Art Basel Miami Beach	Installation
2014	Tokyo, Japan	"My stuffed Pom Room" in collaboration with CHINTAI, a real estate company	Installation
2014	Japan	A remake of Sanrio's animation movie "Nutcracker"	Art and stage direction
2014	Tokyo, Japan	"Doll Culture Exhibition" at Tokyo City View in Roppongi Hills	Art direction
2014	Tokyo, Japan	"How to Create Your Own Kawaii Monster" at Watarium Art Museum	Workshop and lecture
2014	Los Angeles, USA	Designed NHK International's booth at Anime Expo	Design project
2014	Japan	"Kyary Pamyu Pamyu Cinema John" movie	Art direction

(*Continued*)

Year	Location	Title	Genre
2014	Miami, USA	"Colorful Rebellion-Seventh Nightmare" at the Young at Art Museum	Exhibition
2014	Florida, USA	"What is kawaii?" at the Consulate-General of Japan in Miami	Lecture
2014	New York, USA	"The Colorful Rebellion–Seventh Nightmare" at Kianga Ellis Projects (It travelled to Miami, Milan, Amsterdam and Antwerp)	Exhibition
2014	Fukushima, Japan	"Harajuku in Iwaki" in collaboration with Cai Guo-Qiang, a Chinese contemporary artist	Workshop and Event
2014	Aichi, Japan	"Amour du Chocolat" Valentine Fair at Takashimaya Department Store in Nagoya	Art direction
2014	Japan	Nintendo's "Bravery Default For the Sequel" 3DS Software	Design project
2014	Japan	Kyary Pamyu Pamuseum	Art direction
2013	Tokyo, Japan	"Melty-Go-Round Tree" for Christmas at Roppongi Hills	Installation
2013	Tokyo, Japan	"Colorful Rebellion – OCTOPUS-" on top of the CUTE CUBE building in Harajuku	Installation

(Continued)

APPENDIX A

Year	Location	Title	Genre
2013	Japan	Kyary Pamyu Pamyu's "Furisodeshon"	Music video
2012	Japan	Kyary Pamyu Pamyu's "Fashion Monster"	Music video
2012	Japan	Kyary Pamyu Pamyu's "Candy Candy"	Music video
2012	Japan	"Wiz-OZ no Mahoutsukai," a Japanese version of the Broadway musical, The Wizard of OZ	Art direction
2011	Japan	Kyary Pamyu Pamyu's "Tsukematsukeru"	Music video
2011	Japan	Kyary Pamyu Pamyu's "PONPONPON"	Music video
2009	Berlin, Germany	The World Tour	Fashion show, lecture & pop-up store
2009	London, England	The World Tour	Fashion show, lecture & pop-up store
2009	Paris, France	The World Tour	Fashion show, lecture & pop-up store
1995	Tokyo, Japan	6%DOKIDOKI launch	Shop

Source: sebastianmasuda.com

APPENDIX B

Timeline of Sebastian Masuda's Key Events

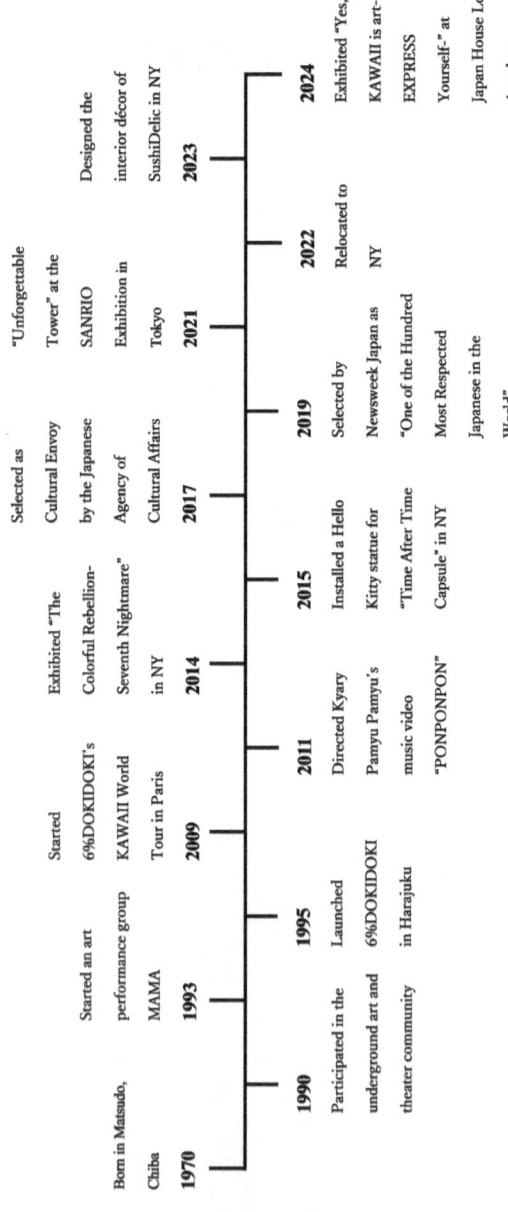

1970 Born in Matsudo, Chiba

1990 Participated in the underground art and theater community

1993 Started an art performance group MAMA

1995 Launched 6%DOKIDOKI in Harajuku

2009 Started 6%DOKIDOKI's KAWAII World Tour in Paris

2011 Directed Kyary Pamyu Pamyu's music video "PONPONPON"

2014 Exhibited "The Colorful Rebellion-Seventh Nightmare" in NY

2015 Installed a Hello Kitty statue for "Time After Time Capsule" in NY

2017 Selected as Cultural Envoy by the Japanese Agency of Cultural Affairs

2019 Selected by Newsweek Japan as "One of the Hundred Most Respected Japanese in the World"

2021 Installed the "Unforgettable Tower" at the SANRIO Exhibition in Tokyo

2022 Relocated to NY

2023 Designed the interior décor of SushiDelic in NY

2024 Exhibited "Yes, KAWAII is art-EXPRESS Yourself." at Japan House Los Angeles

REFERENCES

Al-Jamie, Anthony. "Interview with Sebastian Masuda: Ambassador of Kawaii." *The Tokyo Journal*, no. 275, September 13, 2014. https://www.tokyojournal.com/sections/fashion-design/item/443-sebastian-masuda.

Al-Jamie, Anthony. "King of Kawaii-Sebastian Masuda's World of Kawaii." *The Tokyo Journal*, no. 284, August 23, 2024.

Aoki, Shoichi. *Fresh FRUiTS*. Phaidon, 2005.

Aoki, Shoichi. *FRUiTS*. Phaidon, 2001.

Aoki, Shoichi. *FRUiTS*. Street Editorial Room, 1997–2017.

Ash. "The History of: Decora." *The Comm*, May 31, 2022. https://the-comm.online/blog/the-history-of-decora/.

Blumer, Herbert. "Fashion: From Class Differentiation to Collective Selection." *Sociological Quarterly*, 10(3), 1969: 275–291.

Chapin, Emerson. "When East Meets West: Japanese Call It Kawaii." *The New York Times*, April 20, 1965. https://timesmachine.nytimes.com/timesmachine/1965/04/20/issue.html.

Corradi, Richard B. "The Repetition Compulsion in Psychodynamic Psychotherapy." *The Journal of American Academy of Psychoanalysis and Dynamic Psychiatry*, no. 37, 2009: 477–500, doi:10.1521/jaap.2009.37.3.477.

Depth. "Interview with Sebastian Masuda." Edition 05, December 17, 2024.

Depth. "Interview with Sebastian Masuda." Edition 02, May 11, 2024.

Disney Fan. "Disney Fan Meets: Sebastian Masuda." Kodansha, October 2019.

Emani, Roghiye, Haleh Ghavami, Moloud Radfar, Hamid Reza Khalkhali. "Impact of Chromotherapy on Professional Quality of Life in Intensive Care Unit Nurses: A Randomized Controlled Trial." *Fatigue: Biomedicine, Health & Behavior*, 8(3), 2020: 121–129. doi:10.1080/21641846.2020.1782058.

Fabricant, Florence. "Sushidelic Embraces Kawaii with Neon Pink Styling and Individual Sushi Bites." *The NY Times*, June 20, 2023. https://www.nytimes.com/2023/06/20/dining/nyc-restaurant-news-openings.html.

Fashion Tech News. "Interview with Sebastian Masuda: Kawaii ga Sekai ni ataeta Eikyou towa (The Impact that Kawaii Has Given to the World)." December 20, 2024. https://fashiontechnews.zozo.com/features/features009/sebastian_masuda.

Fujii, Ryo. "Interview with Sebastian Masuda." *Getnews*, March 3, 2014. https://getnews.jp/archives/525572.

Garfinkel, Harold. *Studies in Ethnomethodology*. Routledge, 1991.

Hobo Nikkan Itoi Shimbun. "Sebastian Masuda in conversation with Shigesato Itoi." December 18–30, 2015. https://www.1101.com/sebastian.

Iwabuchi, Koichi. *Recentering Globalization: Popular Culture and Japanese Transnationalism.* Duke University Press, 2002.

Jonauskaite, Domicele, Ahmad Abu-Akel, and Christine Mohl. "Universal Patterns in Color-Emotion Associations are Further Shaped by Linguistic and Geographic Proximity." *Psychological Science*, 31(10), 2020: 1245–1260. doi: 10.1177/0956797620948810.

Jonetsu Tairiku, "Kyary Pamyu Pamyu," a documentary program on TBS, February 27, 2012. https://www.youtube.com/watch?v=JGewNtv7HVQ.

Kawamura, Yuniya. *Fashioning Japanese Subcultures: Decentralization and Diversification as Neotribes.* 2nd edition. Bloomsbury, 2025.

Kawamura, Yuniya. *The Japanese Revolution in Paris Fashion.* Berg, 2004.

Levine, Howard B. "The Compulsion to Repeat: An Introduction." *The International Journal of Psychoanalysis*, no. 101, 2020: 1162–1171. doi: 10.1080/00207578.2020.1815541.

Masuda, Sebatian, "111 years of Junichi Nakahara," The Junichi Nakahara Exhibition Catalogue, Sogo Art Museum, 2023.

Masuda, Sebastian. "My NY Diary: I am Still a Newcomer." March 25, 2022. https://note.com/sebastea/n/n99b965b33522.

Masuda, Sebastian. "My NY Diary: Viva La Vida." February 16, 2022. https://note.com/sebastea/n/n7817ecdee5e8.

Masuda, Sebastian. *Sekai ni Hitotsudake no Kawaii no Mitsuke Kata* (How to Find Only One "Kawaii" in the World), Sunmark Publishing, 2018.

Masuda, Sebastian. *Kakeizu Katta* (The Family Tree Cutter). Kadokawa Publishing, 2011.

Matsunaga, Rei. "Interview with Sebastian Masuda – to Live a life true to one's self, with determination," Telling. *Asahi Shimbun*, March 14, 2019.

McRobbie, Angela. *Feminism and Youth Culture: From "Jackie" to "Just Seventeen"*. Macmillan, 1991: xv.

Ministry of Health, Labour and Welfare, The. "Suicide Rates." https://www.mhlw.go.jp/stf/seisakunitsuite/bunya/hukushi_kaigo/seikatsuhogo/jisatsu/jisatsu_year.html.

Mizushima, Nanae. "No. 97 Interview: Sebastian Masuda-Kawaii Is a Concept, and Not about Things". *Roppongi Mirai Kaigi*, September 26, 2018. https://6mirai.tokyomidtown.com/en/interview/97/.

Newsweek Japan. "The Hundred Most Respected Japanese in the World." April 30–May 7 issue, 2019. https://www.newsweekjapan.jp/magazine/238541.php.

Nye, Joseph. *Soft Power: The Means to Success in World Politics*. Public Affairs, 2004.

REDAC. "Interview with Sebastian Masuda (in Japanese)." EXPAT Channel, 2023. https://www.youtube.com/watch?v=xKyJvIn9kbg.

Ronin Gallery. "Sebastian Masuda Forments a Kawaii Rebellion at Ronin Gallery." October 28, 2016. https://www.artsy.net/article/artsy-sebastian-masuda-foments-a-kawaii-rebellion-at-ronin-gallery-in-new-york.

Rose, Megan Catherine. "Kawaii Affective Assemblages. Cute New Materialism in Decora Fashion Harajuku." *The Journal of Media Studies*, 25(4), October 5, 2022. https://doi.org/10.5204/mcj.2926.

Takeshita, Ikuko. "Interview with Sebastian Masuda." *Business Insider Japan*, June 5, 2019. https://www.businessinsider.jp/article/191847/.

Terayama Shuji. *Showo Suteyo, Machie Deyo* (Throw Away Your Books and Rally in the Streets). Kadokawa, 1971.

University of Tennessee at Chattanooga. "What Is Kawaii- Lecture by Sebastian Masuda." July 3rd, 2014. https://www.youtube.com/watch?v=PTc_I825Gak.

Valdez, Patricia, and Albert Mehrabian. "Effects of Color on Emotions." *The Journal of Experimental Psychology: General*, 123(4), 1994: 394–409. https://doi.org/10.1037/0096-3445.123.4.394.

Van der Kolk, Bessel. "The Compulsion to Repeat the Trauma: Reenactment, Revictimization, and Masochism." *Psychiatric Clinics of North America*, no. 12, 1989: 389–411.

Van der Kolk, Bessel A., and Charles P. Ducey. "The Psychological Processing of Traumatic Experience: Rorschach Patterns in PTSD." *Journal of Traumatic Stress*, no. 2, 1989: 259–274.

Wall Street Journal. "Contemporary Kawaii Is Flourishing – There Is No Japanese Word for Cloying." February 21, 1986.

Welms, Lisa, and Daniel Oberfeld. "Colors and Emotion: Effects of Hue, Saturation and Brightness." *Psychological Research*, 82, 2017: 896–914. DOI: 10.1007/s00426-017-0880-8.

Werner, Laurie. "This Whimsical Sushi Bar Is Now The Hottest Restaurant In New York." *Forbes*, June 29, 2023. https://www.forbes.com/sites/lauriewerner/2023/06/29/this-whimsical-sushi-bar-is-now-the-hottest-restaurant-in-new-york/.

WWD Japan. "Harajuku New Era: People Who Connect Fashion and Culture." April 22, 2024.

Yanagita, Kunio. *Tono Monogatari*. Aozora Bunko, 1910.

INDEX

accomplishments xvi, xvii, 60, 66, 67, 85
ambition 34, 35, 92, 98
anniversary xv, 28, 68
anxiety xxi, 29, 56n2
apartment 15, 94
attachment xxii, 9, 11, 35

business 2, 6, 12, 23, 31, 34, 44

café 52
carpenter 18, 30, 107
childish madness 20
collaborations 43
colors, vibrant/neon/psychedelic xv, xvi, xviii, xxi, 28, 31, 41, 50, 51, 60, 61, 63–65, 73, 75, 86, 88, 91, 92, 100–2, 105–7
consignment 34
contradictions xxv
contributions 60
cultural diplomacy xvi, xxiv, 60, 84

Decora xix, xxiii, 35, 39, 41, 44, 51, 60, 78, 86, 88, 102
disappointment 14
dokidoki 62

ESMOD 44, 58n21
ethnomethodology 22

faith 6, 8, 85
fashion shows xxiii, 39, 61, 78
friendship 12, 40
FRUiTS 37, 57n10, 57n12

Ginza xix, 56
Gonzales 19
grandmother 2, 5, 8, 9

hikikomori 13, 26n13
hometown xxi, xxii, 11, 36, 50, 106

identity xxv, 18, 36, 83
ideology xvii, xxv, 61, 88

Jinju Bridge 39

kimono xxii, 2, 5, 6, 23, 62
Kyary Pamyu Pamyu xxiii, xxvin7, 50, 58n25, 71, 86, 119, 121
Kyushu 34

lineage xx, 4
Lolita xix, 35, 39
Los Angeles xxiii, xxiv, 30, 69, 74, 76, 89n4, 89n15, 99, 107, 110, 116, 119

MAMA 19–21, 28
Matsudo xxi, 2, 18, 25n2, 36, 50, 113
merchandise 29, 31, 37, 68
modernization 43
My Little Pony 33, 57n6

New York xv, xvi, xvii, xviii, xxi, xxiii, xxiv, 36, 42, 54, 56n1, 58n17, 70, 72, 73, 75, 78–80, 84, 85, 92–94, 97, 100, 101, 109–11, 115, 116, 118, 120

obstacles 66, 91, 94
Omotesando 11, 40, 57n14
Osaka xxii, 12–14, 31, 34, 49, 54, 58n21, 90n18, 106, 110–12, 114, 117

pandemic xxiv, 54, 76, 80, 91, 92
peace 91, 99, 107
philosophy xv, xvii, xxiii, xxv, 15, 16, 20, 22, 34, 35, 42, 59, 61, 68, 73, 77, 103
policemen 21
pop-up stores xxiii, 97
psychology 9, 63, 65

rent xxi, xxiii, 1, 2, 5, 6, 8, 9, 11, 13, 18, 24, 25, 26n6, 26n18, 28, 30, 31, 35, 38, 41, 44, 50, 54, 63, 69, 70, 73, 81, 82, 87, 88, 92–94, 97, 101
reputation xxii, 15, 33, 34, 37, 54, 59

secondhand clothes xxiii, 30
sensational kawaii 29, 33
Shibuya xix, xxii, 11, 12, 34, 40
Shinjuku xix, xxii, 18
shopgirls 68
shopping arcade xxi, 34, 40, 105
siblings xx, 2, 5, 31
soft power xxiii, 60, 82
stupidity 19, 20
surgery 8
sushi restaurant 54, 78, 90n18, 99, 110

INDEX

Takenoko-zoku 36
Takeshita Street 39, 40
television 18, 30, 107
toys xxi, 31, 44, 48, 51, 65, 73, 100, 107
trauma reenactment 9, 10

Ura-hara 29

vaccinations 55

Warhol, Andy 28, 56n1
westernization 43
workshop 69, 100

www.ingramcontent.com/pod-product-compliance
Lightning Source LLC
Chambersburg PA
CBHW032027230426
43671CB00005B/229